INDIANS OF
COO-YU-EE PAH
(PYRAMID LAKE)

THE HISTORY OF THE
PYRAMID LAKE INDIANS IN NEVADA

INDIANS OF COO-YU-EE PAH (PYRAMID LAKE)

THE HISTORY OF THE PYRAMID LAKE INDIANS IN NEVADA

by
Nellie Shaw Harnar

KEYSTONE
CANYON PRESS

KEYSTONE
CANYON PRESS

Keystone Canyon Press
2341 Crestone Drive
Reno, NV 89523

www.keystonecanyon.com

Editor Alrica Goldstein
Cover Design Alissa Booth

Library of Congress Control Number: 2023946205

ISBN: 978-1-953055-32-3
Epub ISBN: 978-1-953055-33-0

Manufactured in the United States of America

Dedication

To the memory of my husband, Curtis S. Harnar, who gave me so many years of faithful, loving companionship and who supported me in my efforts to make this book possible.

To the memory of my· father and mother who endowed me with pride in my race and heritage, and for their sacrifices and encouragement that I might obtain an education.

To my son, Curtis Harnar, and grandchildren, Charles Curtis and Craig Curtis Hamar, I affectionately dedicate this book, with the hope it will in some way be an inspiration to them.

Nellie Shaw Hamar

Contents

Foreword

Many nineteenth-century writings reveal the white man's respect for the Northern Paiute Indians of Northwestern Nevada. Documents written during the eighteen hundreds show an amazing unanimity of opinion regarding the morality, integrity, and industry of the desert people.

Twentieth-century writers have recorded, both in scientific papers and layman publications, portions of the history and culture of these Native Americans. But now we have something of special interest, a book written by a Northern Paiute Indian woman about her own people.

Mrs. Nellie Shaw Harnar, for many years a highly respected teacher at the Stewart Indian School, began her book as her thesis for her Masters Degree at the University of Nevada. Written in a pleasant, easily-read style, her story of her people soon began to show her pride in her heritage. And there is solid historical evidence to warrant such pride—something I would like to consider for the remainder of this foreword.

National Archives Microfilms, California newspaper files, U.S. Senate Documents, U.S. Army and Indian Affairs reports, and Nevada histories have furnished the following quotations which, taken together, create an interesting picture of the Northern Paiute during this early period. The following quotations are arranged in chronological order.

1859

In 1859, Captain J. S. Simpson, in his Report of Explorations Across the Great Basin of the Territory of Utah, recorded information furnished him by Indian Agent, Major Frederick Dodge.

"The Pi-Ute (Paiute) nation number from 6,000 to 7,000 souls. They inhabit western Utah (Utah territory in 1859 included Nevada) . . . They are divided into bands about 200 strong each, commanded by a Subchief. The head chief of the nation is Wan-a-muc-a (The Giver). The largest portion of the nation is generally to be found in the vicinity of the principal rivers and lakes of the Great Basin: Humboldt, Carson, Walker, Truckee, Owens, Pyramid, and Mono. The Pi-Utes resemble in appearance, manner and customs, the Delawares of our Missouri frontier, and with judicious management and assistance from the General Government, they would equal in three years their brother Delawares in agricultural and other advancements made by them toward civilization."

U.S. Senate Documents of the 1859-60 36th Congress recorded Major Frederick Dodge's belief that, "The Paiutes are undoubtedly the most interesting . . . Indians on the continent."

1860

Early observers described these desert people of Western Nevada as tall, with long, thin faces. The Pyramid Lake leader, Numaga (Young Winnemucca) was said to be 6 feet 4 inches in height. A Sacramento newspaper reporter who interviewed him in 1860, wrote, "Numaga is not just a superior Indian; he is a superior man of any race."

In April of 1860, S. Stanbaugh, Surveyor General of Utah Territory, wrote the Commissioner of the U.S. General Land Office that the Paiutes, "are represented as being a very industrious and peaceable people."

The two battles of Pyramid Lake took place in May and June of 1860, and there were many written accounts praising the battle tactics, horsemanship, skill with weapons, and bravery of the Paiute warriors. The Sacramento Daily Union and Sacramento Bee newspapers of May and June, 1860, contain many descriptive accounts. Colonel John C. Hays, commanding the army of regulars and volunteers in the second battle of Pyramid Lake, is quoted as saying that the Paiutes shot better than he had ever seen Indians shoot; and he claimed that the warriors were "beautifully mounted" and "rode splendidly."

In August and September of 1860, Colonel F. W. Lander, superintendent of the Overland Wagon Road, attempted to bring peace to the territory through which emigrants to California traveled. His lengthy report with enclosures, to the Commissioner of Indian Affairs is recorded on National Archive Microfilm and contains many personal observations of the Paiute Indians. Several quotations from the report, selected because of the interest and their indication of the innate dignity of the Paiute fellow.

Colonel Lander met with the Paiute war chief Numaga (Young Winnemucca), at the Hot Springs on the emigrant road near the Humboldt Sink. "They arrived there early in the day designated, bringing with them the chief and four of his principal warriors."

"Winnemucca said he would look hard at me and when the sun was low would be ready to talk. The council, which was held at sunset, lasted over an hour and was quite an interesting one. . . .

"His reply was characteristic of the better class Indians of the plains. He said that when he asked me to wait until night before he would talk in a former report, are the most quiet and tractable people I have ever met with and are easily managed when kindly and judiciously treated. As a people they are honest, amiable and friendly. It is a rare thing; to find one among them who will commit a theft upon the whites or upon one of their own people . . ."

1865

Franklin Campbell, Indian Agent of the Walker River Indian Reservation, on June 9, 1865, wrote the Commissioner of Indian Affairs in Washington, D.C., as follows: "I have been the local Indian Agent on this reserve since April 1st, 1862 up to the present time, fifteen months, excepted. This constant life among the Pi-Utes has enabled me to become acquainted with them both personally and generally throughout the tribe, and also to form opinions based on experience as to their true character, better perhaps than any other man in the State.

"On the whole they are as honest, and truthful as the whites, but they lack organization and law. They are good reasoners and thinkers and are generally kind and humane . . . l do say the material is here for a high standard of civilization.

"As yet they have resisted the harmful influences of intoxicating drink and have preserved with great tenacity the native virtue of their women.

"They are willing to work and exhibit considerable industry in gaining a livelihood in this desert country. Many of them have been to California and have learned to do all kinds of farm work. These are extremely anxious to cultivate their lands if they only get the necessary supplies and have them applied . . ."

1867

On December 8, 1867, U.S. Major H. Douglas, Superintendent of Indian Affairs in Nevada, wrote E. S. Parker, Commissioner of Indian Affairs in Washington, D.C., "They (Paiutes) make money enough to obtain food and clothing by working at small jobs such as chopping and sawing wood, tending stock, shooting ducks for which they find a ready market, and other transient occupations. They appear to be well fed and comfortably clothed by their own efforts without any assistance from Government.

"Though in almost continual contact with whites, gambling appears to be the only vice to which they are addicted. Cases of drunkenness are extremely rare. Unlike the Indians of the Plains and the Eastern Border, they are willing to work for a compensation and comparatively, though unaided by Government, they are in a much better condition than those Indians."

"Whether Indians can be induced of their own free will to remain permanently on the Reservation allotted to them is questionable; they may be so persuaded, provided it is made clearly apparent to them that it is to their advantage to do so."

Reports of the Commissioner of Indian Affairs contain many references to the Northern Paiutes. Several quotations have been selected which indicate the Paiute's ability to adapt to a changing environment without loss of morality or integrity.

1871

REPORT OF the Commissioner of Indian Affairs for 1871, page 558, contains a statement that the Paiute Indians were, "superior in intelligence and culture."

Page 559 includes, "Their manifest regard for their females is remarkable indeed . . . I have been told repeatedly that of the more than 5,000 Paiute Indians, there is not a mixed blood among them and I have seen nothing to contradict it."

1876

In 1876, Dan DeQuille (William Wright) wrote in *The Big Bonanza*, "Very few Paiutes will touch whiskey or liquor of any kind. The women are remarkable for their chastity, and are in this respect models . . . for those of all nations and colors."

1880

The 1880 Report of the Comissioner of Indian Affairs, page 123, describes the Walker River Paiutes as, "peaceful, intelligent, agricultural, people."

1883

Page 11, of *The Report of the Commissioner of Indian Affairs For 1883*, states that the Pyramid Lake Paiutes, "seem endeavoring to conform to the existing order of things and are making efforts to learn the use of tools in every line, especially they take to blacksmithing."

1887

Page 162, of *The Report of the Commissioner of Indian Affairs, 1887,* describes the Paiutes as "with very few exceptions, peaceable, quiet, lawabiding, tractable, sober and industrious, doing much hard work to place their little farms in a condition for advantageous cultivation . . ."

1898

The 1898 Report of the Commissioner of Indian Affairs, page 379, contains, "There is a legend among these Indians, and I presume it can be considered a historical fact, for it is verified by citizens of this community, to the effect that virtue among the Paiute women was an established and absolute fact."

1904

Thomas Wren, in his *History of Nevada*, published in 1904, wrote, "It is an old saying that thieves, cowards, and lewd women are never found among the Paiutes."

"The Paiutes have a long face, rather narrow, and a wonderful cranium development . . . There is nothing a Paiute cannot learn, and they are gifted with wonderful powers of oratory. This is proved in the schools on the reservation . . . the Paiute is good in both physical and mental tasks . . . The teachers become greatly attached to their pupils . . . some of the Indians have graduated and in their time become teachers . . . are extremely loyal to their employers."

1963

Frank McCullock, Sr., a former rancher in the Fernley District, spent much of his life near the Paiute Indians. He spoke their language and worked with them on the range. In a letter dated December 11, 1963, he wrote:

"I came to Wadsworth, Nevada in 1899 with my parents and went to work on a ranch for 'Old Man Olinghouse', discoverer of the Olinghouse gold mines, as a chore boy on his ranch. After some years—1902, I think—my father bought out the old man's cattle outfit in the Fox Mountains and for some 6 years I was cattle boss for him on the range.

"We used only Indians as cow hands . . .

"Indians like Jigger Bob, Updike, Sam Kay, Bobby Dodd, and oh, so many others, dead and gone years ago . . .

"I can only say that the Indians whose names I have quoted were just about the finest men I have ever known. They were heroes to me then, they still are today."

The Native Americans can be proud of their heritage.

SESSIONS S. "BUCK" WHEELER
April, 1978

CHAPTER I

Northern Paiute Land
(Neh-muh Tubewah)

The Pyramid Lake Indian land was a small tract compared to the larger one tribally used and claimed.

In 1828, this Neh-muh Tubewah was still intact. That Northern Paiute homeland had been entered by few, if any, Caucasians. It was named the Great Basin country by Captain John C. Frémont. The Rocky and the Sierra Nevada Mountains encased this arid land. This low moisture area extended to the north beyond the aforementioned ranges. This was the Neh-muh Tubewah.

The Neh-muh knew the locations where the fresh waters and food, both plant and animal, were available. Utilizing natural resources, they practiced the art of conservation and preservation and were satisfied with the results.

The bands of the Northern Paiute extended into the modern states of Oregon, Idaho, California, and Nevada. Each band was an entity, a small group of individuals who chose to live together in a specific locale, although sometimes a single member or family traveled outside the band region. It was not uncommon for bands to group together at certain times for games and to gather food in season. A band was named according to the abundance of a specific food available, or to the location of the band home area. The Atsu ku dok wa (Red Mountain),[1] the Yamosopo and the Sawa wak to do bands located in the Humboldt River area were first contacted by the early British fur trappers. The Kupa band lived in the Humboldt Sink area while the Toe band was located at the Carson Sink. In the Walker Lake area was the Agai Dokado (trout eater) band.

The Ku yui Pah (Pyramid Lake) area was widely known for the abundance of the Ku yui and agai fish. Thence, came the neighboring band members at the spawning time of the fish, which usually coincided with the depletion of their

NUMANA DAVE (Numana, Father to the Neh-muh) Police Captain
and last of the early great Pyramid Lake Chiefs. 1833(?) – 1919

own stored food. These visits demonstrated the Indians' love for family reunions and feasts. These gatherings also constituted a means of introducing the young people to each other under the watchful eye of "matchmaking" parents.

North of the Ku yui Pah were the Kamo, the Kidu, and the Agai Panina areas while to the west were the Taseget and Wada land, to the south were the Tovusi and Pakwi Bands.

In this Tubewah the Paiutes diligently conserved nature; they fully realized that life depended on it. They religiously used the animals, plants, and water for their way of living.

The fire for cooking was a small one; dry fuel was from the sage, greasewood, cottonwood, or willow; and for kindling, the sage bark, or small dry branches were used. Stones around or in the fire helped to hold the heat but when there was no more use for the fire, it was covered with sand to prevent spreading.

Only a small area was cleared for the canee (wickiup or teepee). The cleared brush was used as shelter at the sides of the doorway, and when dry was used for firewood or the bark used for clothing, should it be sagebrush.

Sometimes if brush, tule, or tree shelters were abandoned they could be reused. However, if they were sites of sickness or death, they were burned; in this fashion sanitation was maintained.

In gathering the wild onion[2] the leaves were utilized. The bulbs were left in the ground, however. If the bulbs were taken then some onions were left for the next season's growth.

Part of the roots of the medicinal plants were left in the ground for the next year's growth. An example is the wild Morning Glory (hermidium alipes (hé wo vy)).

The sagebrush (artemisia or tridentata (sa wá be)) were gainfully used by the Paiutes, and though it grew profusely in the habitat it was never deliber- ately destroyed. The bark was used for jackets, trousers, shirts, blouses, shoes, mattresses for babies, twine, and kindling wood. The leaves were used for tonics. Many times the whole plant was used for shelter.

Though the Paiutes were seed gatherers, they would not take all the seeds. They thus left the root and plant intact while pinching off the seedpods which they put into the closely woven burden baskets.

The balsam (sagittata (ah kuh) and the sand grass (hymenoid (wye)) produced seed food for the Paiutes. When the wild sweet potato (carum gairdneri (Ya pah)), the sego lily bulb (nultallii (kogi)), and other helpful roots were dug from the ground, a thank you was said or given when the soil was returned to the hole. The old people reverently said, "May more plants grow here." Sometimes dry plants were also put into the hole and covered. The younger ones would put a piece of cloth or a toy into the cavity before it was closed.

The large game killed was practically all utilized. The flesh and internal organs were divided among band members. The skin was used for clothing, shelter lining, or bed covering. Of the small animals the rabbit meat was used for food while the skin was for clothing and blankets.

From the willow, a very beneficial plant to the Paiutes, only select branches were taken. They were used for baby cradles, seed gathering baskets, cooking baskets, hats, water jugs, winnowing baskets, spoons, and shelter.

The pine nut (pinon (tuba)) was one of the staple foods for the Paiute. Care was taken that the tree was uninjured in the process of nut harvesting. Only the cones were taken down from the trees. The underbrush of the tree was removed to make the seed gathering easier and to prevent forest fires. The old limbs under the trees were used for firewood.

The Paiute comprehended that the conservation and preservation of nature was essential to his existence.

All the bands had their own legends as storytelling was for entertaining and preserving the tribal lore.

Two Kuyui Dokado legends are the Stone Mother and the Water Babies at Coo yu ee Lake.

Stone Mother

Long ago in the Great Basin lived one large family. This was known as the Neh-muh family or the Northern Paiutes as they are known today.

These people were gentle and kind, but one brother was quarrelsome. He swayed some of his sisters and brothers to his bad manners. The children then divided into two sides. There was a continuous bickering from day to day that led to blows, counter· blows, and much physical harm.

When the parents saw that their counseling was of no avail they decided to separate the children. This was a bitter decision, but had to be taken before murder was committed.

The father told the children that they had to move away from the parental home. He designated the quarrelsome leader to the land over the tall Sierra Mountains into what today is California. This brother and his family became the Pitt River Indians.

A brother who favored the quarrelsome one was designated to the land in the cold north—today's Idaho. He and his group became the Bannocks.

Another brother was asked to go to the southland beyond the Sierra Nevada to Owen's Valley in modern California. These became known as the

Paiute Willow Baskets
Pine Pitch Covered Water Jug, Owner, Margie Shaw, 1927;
Beaded Basket, Maker, Jennie Williams, 1924.

southern Paiutes or the Pe tah neh quad.

Others of this family were dispersed into bands to lands near rivers and lakes.

The parents remained but were very sad. They were truly heartbroken when the Pitt River band returned to fight the remaining groups.

The father passed on to the Great Milky Way. Then there seemed no consolation for the wife and mother. Even at her chores of seed gathering she wailed and mourned. No one checked her whereabouts when she did not return to her canee at night.

Notice was made only when a large body of salt water appeared. Near this pah nun a du was the form of the mother. She still had her burden basket on her back. She had been turned to a stone. The lake was the tears she had shed.

The Stone Mother is one of the Coo yu e Lake's tufa formations. It can be seen close to the Woh noh (Pyramid) today.

The area around the Stone Mother is a sacred place to the Neh-muh for their meditation and prayer.

Water Babies at Coo-yu-ee Lake

In the Long Ago, the Neh-muh traded with the Indians living beyond the snow-clad mountains to the West (Sierra Nevada). Generally, these traders were composed of groups of men only. But occasionally, they took their families with them.

One party of traders, after visiting several tribes in the Land near the Ocean made ready to return to the Neh-muh country.

One of their members was not accounted for so they waited over for several days. The youth never reappeared. Finally, the leader decided that the return home would have to be made with or without his presence. That evening, they remained in camp longer than usual in the hopes that the absent one would overtake them.

Several nights later the young man did appear. They were exultant at the sight of him. Although overjoyed at the reunion, the straggler was noticeably depressed.

The other traders exchanged tales of their adventure, but the youth made no comment. As the evening progressed into night, one by one the people retired. When only the leader and the youth remained, the leader asked, "Is there something you would like to tell me?" After a long moment the youth answered in the affirmative, and revealed he was planning to bring a wife back with him. The leader was not too surprised, and said, "Bring her to our camp so that we can all leave together in the morning."

The groom then left to fetch his bride as the leader waited to welcome them. He was astounded when the youth emerged bearing a mermaid in his arms. After the leader designated a place for the young couple to stay that night, he beckoned the husband and he begged him to return the wife to her home. The young man replied that he loved her and wanted to take her to his home in the Neh-muh country.

Because he was persistent, the leader retired filled with misgivings. Before falling asleep he pictured the troubles the pair would encounter. The Neh-muh people did not relish the idea of strange wives for their young men as the mother in the Neh-muh family was its head, and they would certainly doubly resent a Woman-from-the-Sea.

After a restless night the leader got up early to inform the others of the new woman traveler in their midst.

None of the group would consent to taking the girl back to their homeland. One after another they tried to persuade the husband to return her to the sea. Some men volunteered to help him return her to her own home. After each night of the new couple's stay the men found that much water was beginning to surround the camp. Each morning they found it was necessary to move briskly ahead of the ever encroaching water. Eventually the frightened leader decided to tell the pair that they must remain behind, as they were endangering the lives of the other tribal members in the party.

The majority hurried home in the hope that they would never see the mermaid again!

Days passed!

Then one morning the groom arrived with his bride at the village. News of the strange woman had been spread throughout band. The people were terrified!

As kind and friendly as were the Neh-muh, they were also'superstitious. They could not allow a Woman-of-the-Sea to live with them. The chiefs demanded that the relatives refuse to permit the young couple to live with them.

As the young couple advanced, water was already trickling in their wake. This was even more alarming! When the relatives insisted the couple moved to the outskirts of the village.

Those who visited the couple reported a body of water appeared close by the domicile of the newlyweds, and that the bride spent much time immersed. Later the relatives, in apprehension, stopped their visitations altogether.

Today the descendants of the couple may be encountered at the north of the Coo-yu-ee Pah. Water baby crying has been heard, small children's foot tracks have been seen on the beaches, and they themselves have been visible on many occasions.

Since the mother was not accepted by the Neh-muh, in retaliation she cast a spell over her babies and her abode. If any Neh-muh sees these water babies he may become very ill and may even die. To counteract the spell the Neh-muh prays to the Great Spirit to be cleansed of the spell.

Only individual medicine men (poo ha gum) can communicate with the water babies who are their medicine-helpers.

Lake Tahoe was created when the travelers camped with the bride and groom, the Truckee River was created on their journey, and Coo-yu-ce Pah was created at the final residence of the couple.

CHAPTER II

Cultural Background of the Kuyui Dokado Band

The Indians near Pyramid Lake were the Kuyui Dokado band whose Paiute tribal status is controversial.[3] These Indians and other Basin Paiutes originally called themselves Neh-muh. The "Numa" (Neh-muh) was reported by G. W. Ingalls, Indian agent in 1873, as a large group of Indians comprised of many tribes or bands, which were known among themselves and by other Indians by many different names taken from the land they occupied.[4] Neh-muh is the Paiute name for *The People*. Omer Stewart termed these bands Paiutes, because the Indians call themselves thus. These and other bands in the Basin area are related linguistically and culturally.[5]

The Pyramid Lake band was one of the bands called Paviotso by some writers. The habitat of the Paviotso during the first quarter of the nineteenth century was the same as during the reservation period of the latter part of the century.[6] There were five distinct bands that formed the Paviotso tribe in Nevada. These bands were loosely organized. They lived within well-defined boundaries, but visited other bands often. Willard Z. Park thought the Paviotso considered themselves a distinct group whose "attitude may be regarded as an incipient feeling of nationality."[7] In the Indian affairs report of J. W. Powell and G. W. Ingalls in 1874, the Pyramid Lake group was referred to as Paviotso, though all records in the Indian Department list it as Pah Ute, Pai Ute, or Piute. The report said that the group knew itself by Paviotso and thus was recognized by other tribes.[8] The Pyramid Lake Indians say that the Shoshones called some of the Nevada bands Paviotso, but since it has a slurring connotation, it was never accepted by the group. The word Paviotso was interpreted to mean "Snake" by Sam L. Rogers.[9]

Since the Neh-muh groups in Nevada prefer to be called Paiutes, instead of Paviotso, they are termed the Northern Paiutes, while the original Paiutes of southwestern Utah, nearby southern Nevada and California, and northwestern Arizona are called the Southern Paiutes. They have occupied those areas since before the coming of the whites.

The Paiutes of Nevada were described by one of their agents as of "medium stature, well developed, strong, and intelligent."[10] Their strong physique stemmed from their close contact with nature, their activity of hunting, fishing, and gathering of seeds, roots, fruits, and herbs for medicinal purposes and their mixed diet of meat, fish, ducks, eggs, plant leaves, roots, seeds, and fruit. Traditional songs, dance ceremonies, band environment with much physical activity, and good food were evidence that the Paiutes were a happy, healthy, and intelligent people.

The Pyramid Lake band is named the "Kuyui Dokado," after the Kuyui fish (Chamistes cujua) for which Pyramid Lake is famous. In the spring the fish appear in the Truckee River to spawn. Because it is peculiar to the Pyramid Lake, its name was given to the Lake as Coo-yu-ee Pah and to the group living on the lake shore and along the Truckee River. "Dokado" means "eaters."[11]

The Kuyui Dokado band of the Northern Paiute tribe belongs to the Shoshonean stock. "The Shoshonean stock is one of the largest in the United States. The main area occupied by this stock lies in the interior plateau, and included practically the whole of Nevada."[12] Today the Shoshonean stock is included in the larger Uto-Aztecan linguistic group to which the Paiute belongs.

The Kuyui Dokado band area included the Pyramid and Winnemucca Lakes and the lower Truckee River. On the west, the Virginia City Range was the boundary; on the north, the desert separated them from the Kamo Dokado (Rabbit Eater Band); on the east the Kupa Dokado (Ground Squirrel Band) country, and they were bounded on the south by the Truckee Meadows.[13]

Band living consisted of many family groups which recognized the mother as the head of the family; however, a male of character was the Kuyui Dokado band leader. He might inherit the leadership, but if he was not intelligent enough, another leader could be acknowledged. This was done politely by asking another to consider leadership. Care was taken not to injure the pride of anyone, and the weak (or senile) leader was replaced in a kindly way. The leader's knowledge consisted of religious ceremonies and mythology. He was considered the leader because of his age and experience. The people listened to him with respect. Yet for specific occasions, a specialized or more qualified leader commanded the affairs, so that the most experienced, most daring, and most able headed the antelope hunt.[14] Thus leadership in the Kuyui Dokado band was divided among the mother of the family, an elder male of the band, and the specialized leaders of activities.

At the birth of a child in the Kuyui Dokado band, the father customarily ran in any direction each day for ten days. On a running trip he had

Melvin Smith and Corbett Pancho, Ku Yui Dokado young men.
Picture taken with Coo-Yu-ee – Pyramid Lake (Coo Yu ee Pah), Nevada.
Courtesy of Flora Smith

to return with water. Then he took a bath in the sweat house at which he could be assisted by another man, or he might take his bath in the river or lake. At the end of the observance he discarded his old clothes, and was painted with red clay. When he went hunting, he was required to distribute his first kill of game to others; he was forbidden meat, salt, smoking, and gambling at this time.[15]

All babies were regarded as prizes. Girls were as welcome as boys, as they would some day head families. The Kuyui Dokado surmised that the parents of a daughter and their relatives would never be hungry in her home, but in a son's home, the daughter-in-law might not welcome her in-laws. Twins were cared for if they were born, but they were not a topic for joking as caring for them was too burdensome. Another mother might volunteer to help feed one of the twins. Usually the twins were kept together as there was a belief that separated children would grieve and die.[16]

The children were seldom slapped or spanked. After babyhood the children were admonished by shaming and threat. They were taught to work early in childhood, and small baskets were made for them to carry on food-gathering trips. The parents and grandparents helped to teach them to be industrious and to learn the culture of their band. Orphans and impoverished children were adopted by relatives or by other families.

Puberty was a time of important traditional ceremony. A girl was in the charge of her mother and women relatives. She fasted, got up early, ran each day for five days to get water or wood. She was busy with chores, but she was secluded. After that time she was bathed, attired in new clothing, and participated in the prayer ceremony.[17] A boy at puberty was taught the responsibilities of manhood by the father and other men. He fasted, and could not eat of his first kill. Even before puberty he was not permitted to eat of his first kill, because it was believed if he did he would not be successful hunter. At the bath, prayers were given for the youth. He too, was given new clothing.[18]

At first, the young people at marriage went near the wife's family to make their home. Parents or older relatives betrothed the young people.[19] Care was taken that they were not closely related; industry, hunting prowess, gentility, respect in the band were considered when a family was seeking a mate for its child. Invariably the engagement took place while the parties were still quite young. Soon after the girl's puberty ceremony, plans were made for her marriage. Before the marriage the girl was sheltered and kept close to home. One way for her to show interest in the boy chosen for her mate was to serve him water or food; then he in turn took her wrist in approval. The watchful parents recognized the intentions and welcomed the boy.[20]

Since marriage was regarded as sacred, divorce was extremely rare. It was accepted among the Kuyui Dokado only for sterility, incompatibility, and adultery.[21] After a divorce the ex-husband returned to the area of his first home. Children stayed with the mother unless she was ruled incompetent.

There was unity in the band culture, but there was intentional division of responsibilities and duties. Thus older women were revered for their wisdom and allowed to take part in the hunt ceremonies as singers and prayer givers, but only men participated at the male puberty ceremony, at the new fatherhood ceremony, and at the teachings of male young for the hunt. Yet there was a unique bond among all the band.[22]

Band disapproval was so great that each one was obedient to his responsibility of food gathering, hunting. and social position, so that there was no need for police. The band did not fight other bands. The desert area of the Basin was not desired by other Indian tribes. The Northern Paiutes rarely participated in chases and raids as they were too busy for any aggression. When they did, it was defensive.[23]

The Shaman was a part-time specialist in the band and could either be a man or a woman. While not at the hunt, on seed gathering expeditions, building canee (house), or attending other family or band activities, he practiced his songs, prayed to his personal guardian spirit (animal helper) and ghost spirit, if he had one. The shaman prepared his paraphernalia, which was comprised of sticks, feathers (large and small), rattle or rattles, and smoking equipment. Supposedly, a vision gave him his songs, and his power. He practiced while he had the band's approval. As he was in most cases and intelligent and perceptive individual, he often used psychological means to cure the ailing.[24]

Some people were regarded as witches with evil intent. They were feared and not crossed in any way; however, there was no proof that these people actually practiced witchcraft.

An important building used in ceremonials and curing of sickness was the sweat house. It was used by invalids, bathers, and the shaman. Men, men and women, or women would use it. Four people could be accommodated at once. It was domed with a willow frame; the hide-covered door could be on any side. Rocks heated outside were brought into the house and put around the patient or bather. Water was poured on the hot rocks to make steam.

Nature provided for the Kuyui Dokado's food, clothing, shelter, and medicine. The diet of fish, plant, and animal was usually enriched by dried and beaten wild cane. Members of the band chewed a gum of the pine pitch, the rabbit brush root and bark, or the rubbery substance from other plant roots. Fish, meat from game, ducks, roots, and berries were dried and kept for the lean days. Medicinal plants were also kept for days of emergency. Animal skins and plants supplied clothing, blankets, mattresses, weapons for hunting, home utensils, and shelters.

Although many early writers who observed the Paiutes wrote that the Indians were too busy gathering food for sustenance to have time for ceremonies and prayer,[25] they apparently were never close to the Paiute way of life. The Paiute was essentially religious and his religion and ceremonies have always been closely connected. The Kuyui Dokado had great respect for nature. They realized there was a supernatural spirit that could be both favorable and destructive. When baths were taken or at the time of the daily washing, a humble prayer was said. When there was a large number of participants, as at preparation for a hunt or pinenut gathering, the whole band danced and participated in the ceremonies. One always "nah-neh-soo-teh-hai" (prays or humbles himself) when entering the lake. The old Indians said to "talk to the lake." It was the way they gave humble thanks and asked for blessings from the lake spirit.[26]

As custom and tradition ruled the lives of the Indians, so funeral customs were followed rigidly. At death, the corpse was removed from the house and prepared with earth paints after washing.[27] The dead was wrapped in his own blanket, and buried in the rocks or with rock covering in the earth of the adjacent hills and mountains. Many burials were along the banks of the Truckee

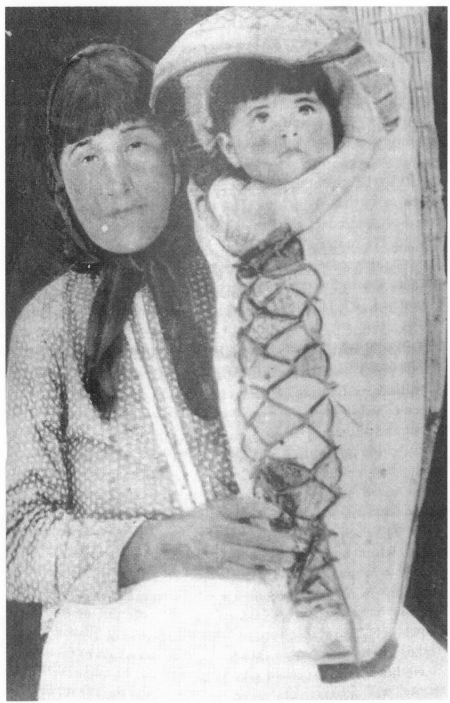

Paiute Mother, Margie Shaw, and daughter
Hube wah taw neh (Nellie) - 1906, Wadsworth, Nevada.

River. The undertaker was a relative or friend. This was an occasion for reverence, gentleness, and great sorrow. Hair clippings were thrown away with ceremony. The women smeared their faces with earth and abstained from washing.
Men refrained from gambling in hand games for three to twelve months. A
widower or widow waited twelve to twenty-four months before remarriage.
Funeral speeches were made by both men and women. Relatives wailed in
loud voices at the funeral; even long afterwards the grieving relatives could be
heard. Gifts were given to the deceased and property of the dead individual
was buried with him. The house in which death occurred was burned or discarded, thus the sickness which caused death would be destroyed. No material
things were kept to renew grieving.

Before contact with the whites, the Paiutes' credo was kindness to all people,
sharing with the hungry and needy, industry, meekness, and reverence.[28] Thus
the Kuyui Dokado and other Paiute bands lived at the time of the Caucasian
intrusion into their Tubewah. Insofar as can be established today, the band
members were happy, independent, and friendly to each other.

CHAPTER III

Intruders and Invaders

Jedediah Smith

The fur trappers, both American and British, were first to intrude into the Paiute homeland. In St. Louis, Jedediah Smith prepared on October 4, 1825, to accompany William H. Ashley beyond the Rockies. He was one of General Ashley's raw recruits, but he was in charge of 70 men, $20,000 worth of outfit, 160 horses and mules. Later, he may have been the first to purposefully travel west on the Oregon Trail.

In the spring of 1827, he was in California searching for a way over the Sierra range. He started east on May 20 with two men, seven horses, two mules loaded with hay and provisions. The travelers went up the north fork of the Stanislaus to Ebbett's Pass, down a route which took them south of Walker Lake in the Neh-muh Tubewah. Two maps he used show he had crossed two streams which were flowing northward. These must have been the East Fork of the Carson River and the West Fork of the Walker River. Passing through the Paiute homeland he noted "When we found water in some of the rocky hills, we most generally found some Indians who appeared the most miserable of human race having nothing to subsist on."[29]

But as he advanced east on June 23, he mentioned killing two hares "which when cooked at night we found much better than horse meat." There was adequate food that the Neh-muh knew of and used, so most of them were well nourished, if not as elaborately dressed as some of the other tribes. The three men having rested at the Springs in Skull Valley were traveling at the base of the Stansbury Mountains when they met with two Indian men, a woman, and two children on July 26, 1827. Though the Indians were surprised, they were friendly and shared their antelope meat with the strangers.

Jedediah, a devout Methodist, were again on the Oregon Trail when, on July 14, 1828, along the banks of the Umpqua River in Southern Oregon there was a plunder of his party. Ten trappers were murdered; rifles and arms were appropriated by the Indians. Smith and two survivors took refuge with the Hudson Bay Company at Ft. Vancouver. Dr. McLoughlin, Superintenent, Pacific Coast of the Company did manage to recover some of the merchandise stolen from the trappers.[30]

There is no record, telling the reason for this attack on a leader who was a respected man among the Mountain people. Nevertheless, intrusion into another's living area, resulting in conflict can be reasonably termed an invasion.

Peter Skene Ogden

When the Hudson Bay Company extended activities into the Snake River country, Peter Skene Ogden, a thirty-year-old trapper was chosen for the exploitation in 1824. He had trapped for beaver in the north and in the Oregon and Idaho areas of today, but not until his Fifth Snake Country Expedition did he venture into the Neh-muh Tubewah of Nevada in the autumn of 1828.

Ogden hurried to the stream he sighted on November 9.[31] There he saw a beaver house that was well stocked. He named the river "Unknown" as he was unaware of either its source or its course. Later, the river was named "Mary's"; then "Paul" to honor the trapper Joseph Paul who died and was buried nearby. Much later Frémont called it Humboldt.

Those trappers came without ever investigating the need the natives themselves might have for the beaver fur in their own country. On November 10, Ogden found the beaver in the Neh-muh Tubewah very wild. On the 13th, he wrote in his Journal that some Indians paid the camp a visit, trading parts of three skins; when asked what had been done with the remainder of the skins, the natives showed their moccasins, which were made from the beaver skins. He then realized why the beaver was so wild.

There were numerous Indians in the area. Many villages line the river, thus from the fires seen at nights in the mountains, the trappers knew they were in the midst of a large band.

One afternoon approximately 150 Neh-muh came to visit. They were described as "miserable looking with scarcely a covering and the greater part were without bows and arrows or any weapons of defence (sic) the only thing I could observe that does them credit, their being fat and in good condition."[32] The Neh-muh were a peaceful people. Only the hunters were equipped with bows and arrows which were used for obtaining game for subsistence, and with the skins they clothed themselves. They were commended for being well fed.

When the beaver traps were being lost, the Indians were blamed for stealing them. Later the trappers reasoned that since the beavers were so wild they got away with some of the traps, for when some traps were found the long dead beavers were still in them. Indians probably took some to reuse in their quest for the same animals.

Ogden returned to the Salt Lake and Rendezvous areas for the winter then retraced the route to the Unknown River in May 1829. Again, Ogden noted Indians were innumerable near the Humboldt Sink. He linked this band to the Pitt Indians of California by the similarity of language and by their friendly advances.[33] He felt they were overly friendly, thereby he indicated a specific spot for them to sit for audience. Since there were so many Indians he was fearful for the safety of his small brigade following.

The Indians of the Humboldt Sink informed the trappers through a Snake interpreter that in eight days travel to the west there was another river flowing to the north from the west; it abounded in salmon but no beaver. They were induced to trade two fish to the trappers to prove they were giving reliable information. They probably were alluding to the Truckee River. Ogden and his men observed these Indians had pieces of ammunition and firearms and other articles which they figured came from Smith's Party which had been attacked in the fall. These articles presumably were traded from Neh-muh to Neh-muh.

Ogden observed the Indians who lived near the swamps used the tule and cattail for food.[34] The roots were eaten fresh in the spring. The leaves were used for clothing, huts, boats, and duck decoys. The sink also contained fish and various species of waterfowl. Duck eggs added to the natives' diet. The fat rabbits were killed in the fall and frozen to be used during the winter and early spring. Seeds gathered in season from various plants and greens were stored for food. In the spring fresh greens were supplemented.

Following the Humboldt to the southwest in early May, Ogden wrote, ". . . I will venture to say in no part of the country have I found Beaver more abundant than in this river and I apprehend we will not soon find another to equal it."[35] When no beaver was found in the Humbold Sink area, Ogden and his followers started to the north over the path they had used in the fall. The journey revealed the depletion of the beaver where they had been so plentiful. Ogden's visit to the Humboldt was finished, but the beaver was so eradicated in this stream the Neh-muh had to find another covering for their feet.

This invasion showed the Caucasian lust for the beaver fur which paid them royally. Their remarks of pity for the poorly clothed Indians were only for record. There were no attempts to solve the natives' living condition by fair trading.

Joseph Reddiford Walker

Another fur trapper to leave a tragic imprint in the Neh-muh Tubewah was Joseph Reddiford Walker. He was a native of Tennessee where he had been a sheriff in Missouri County, then a Santa Fe trader. Walker was one of the assistants to Captain Bonneville when the Captain planned his expedition to the west.

On July 24, 1833, Walker departed from the Grand River to explore the desert area west of Salt Lake. Zenas Leonard, the clerk of the brigade, cited 60 men in the party. He followed closely the route taken by Ogden in 1828 and 1829 from the Great Salt Lake. The trappers were not successful with beaver trapping. They blamed the Indians for thievery of the traps. Some men were so annoyed that when Indians were seen they killed three. Their acts were not revealed to the Captain, but the next time the same violence was committed, the leader heard of it and reprimanded them.[36]

When the party reached the sink they met hundreds of Indians whom they believed to be a war party. However, the Indians left the camp when guns were displayed. The next evening more Indians came and asked to smoke with the trappers, but Walker, fearful of their intentions, ordered 32 of his men to fight. Over thirty Indians were killed, no mention is made of any trappers being slain; yet Walker called this a battle. The Indians were obviously no match for the trappers in this conflict. Walker designated the swamps as "Battle Lakes."

Walker went through the Agai Dokado country, passing their lake and on to the River that today bears his name. He crossed the Sierra by the way of the Tuolumne River and into the San Joaquin Valley of California.[37]

The completion of this exploration signified a new trend of living for the Neh-muh. Thereafter, they were besieged by intrusion and invasion more and more.

On February 14, 1834, the explorers were returning with 52 men, 364 horses, 47 cattle, and 30 dogs. They followed the Kern River up through a pass now known as Walker, then they entered the Humboldt Sink, the "Battle Lakes"; they met the same Indians, only there seemed to be a greater number. The Clerk wrote that gifts were given to the Indians to appease them, but some of the explorers desired to kill all the natives. The Captain then ordered his men into battle formation to attack the Indians in a savage manner. Fourteen Indians were dead and many wounded. Some writers thought this was the only way to subdue the Indians. No other avenue of communication was tried but force to kill. Certainly this is not excusable.

Bonneville, who was responsible for the Walker Expedition, did not sanction the treatment the natives received from Walker and his men.[38]

Henceforth, the Salt Lake, Humboldt River, and Sierra route to California mean that the Neh-much Tubewah was open to outsiders who would pass through or settle on Northern Paiute land. The Indians, thereafter, were to be misrepresented as being universally warlike and unjustly treated as targets immediately on being seen. As time progressed, the Indians had to make many adjustments, some to their advantage and others which were detrimental.

CHAPTER IV

Pyramid Lake Indians in Frémont's Path

The history of the Pyramid Lake Indians in relation to the white man properly begins with Frémont's passage through the area in 1844, but Nevada Indians had encountered white men earlier.

In some instances the earliest encounters between Indians and whites were not friendly. This was particularly true of the experience of the Joseph Reddiford Walker expedition of 1833 as it passed along the Humboldt River on its way to and on his return from California.[39] Evidence indicates that the attack by the whites was unwarranted.[40] Fear on the part of the whites seemed to be the motive for the blows inflicted on the Indians. Although Leonard insisted that the safety of the party required this assault, he realized that the slaughter would not be sanctioned by many others.[41] The historical image of the Indian as a dread savage undoubtedly fed the fears of these early trappers.

Thus the whites had encountered the Nevada Indians in the late 1820's during Ogden's expedition, and certainly in 1833 with the first Walker expedition; but it was not until 1844 that the white man encountered the Pyramid Lake band when Frémont led his second expedition through the Northwest Basin country from Oregon and discovered Pyramid Lake.

Frémont, leader of the first white expedition to visit Pyramid Lake Indians, was born in Savannah, Georgia, on January 21, 1813. At the age of sixteen he entered Charleston College, where he was a good student in mathematics, botany, chemistry, and the classics. Brilliant, but impulsive, restless and unstable, according to his teachers and classmates, he left college three months before he was to graduate.[42] Subsequently, Frémont developed much in common with Missouri Senator Thomas Hart Benton who was interested in the West. Their relationship was cemented by Frémont's marriage to Benton's daughter, Jessie, who was also enthusiastic about the new frontier.

Frémont, on his first expedition to the Far West, explored the Wind River Mountain range in 1842, in what is now Wyoming. He traveled the Platte route on his second expedition, which started in May 1843, and led from Kansas (town), Missouri to Oregon.[43] Then on November 18 of the same year, he prepared to return as ordered.[44] He decided to travel to the South and Southeast so as to explore the Great Basin. One of his missions there was to verify reports of a Mary's Lake which existed in contemporary tales of the region, and a Buenaventura River, which supposedly flowed westward to the Pacific Ocean. The projected line of return was to take him over previously unchartered terrain. Frémont's party consisted of twenty-five men and included Americans, Germans, Canadians, Indians, and one Negro. Many were under twenty-one years of age, and though they knew hardships were to be encountered, they were cheerful, eager, and obedient. The hardships encountered in exploring the new area started at noon on November 25, 1843.[46] As they traveled, on December 28, 1843, the party came upon a camp of eight or ten Indians who ran on to a ridge near the Oregon and Nevada border. They were saying "tai-bo-bo," which meant *White Men* in the Shoshonean dialect.[47] Frémont said that members of this group were as poor as any human beings he had seen, as the people were scantily covered by woven rabbit skins. This was the first Paiute group to be met by Frémont.

Pushing on after meeting the Indian party, Frémont moved south through the area east of present day Cedarville. According to the positions recorded on maps, the supposed position of Mary's Lake and Buenaventura River must have been reached and passed. On January 6, 1844, Frémont; Kit Carson, the famous guide; and Charles Preuss ascended a mountain while Thomas Fitzpatrick explored below. They saw mountain sheep, the steam from a hot spring, and horse tracks near springs surrounded by cottonwood trees.[48]

The spectacular view which they witnessed from a nearby summit on January 10, Frémont described as follows:

> ... filling up all the lower space (was) a sheet of green water, some twenty miles broad. It broke upon our eyes like the ocean ... The waves were curling in the breeze and their dark-green showed it to be a body of deep water. For a long time, we sat enjoying the view, for we had become fatigued with the mountains and the free expanse of moving waves was very grateful.[49]

Because the legendary Mary's Lake had been described as surrounded by open country and meadowy shores, Frémont and Carson decided that they had

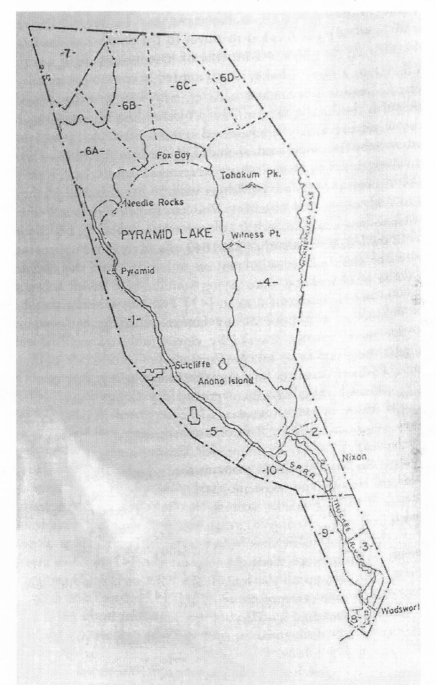

Map of Pyramid Lake Indian Reservation

found an unknown lake. A prominent physical feature of the lake was a rock that jutted from the lake. The men camped opposite it on the night of January 13. They estimated its height to be about six hundred feet above the water. As its outline reminded them of the Pyramid of Cheops in Egypt, Frémont named the body of water Pyramid Lake.[50]

On January 14, 1844, Frémont induced one of the natives who were observing the whites from the high land to come into camp. The Indian and his companions were "poor looking and naked" except for tunics of rabbit skins. The Indian told Frémont and his party of a river, but he could not reveal whether it was an inlet or an outlet. He led the party past the caves where the Indians lived. Baskets and seeds were nearby, but people were nowhere to be seen. The baskets were used for storage, cooking, cradling babies, and for carrying burdens. Horse tracks were also seen near the lake shore.[51]

As the white men approached the mouth of the river, three or four Indians appeared and conversed in a sign language. These Indians were well fed and happy because they were located where there was an abundance of food. Many species of fish in the lake and river were at their disposal. These were supplemented by plant greens, roots, seeds, fruit, and by large animals such as mountain sheep, deer, and antelope. There were numerous small animals such as a rabbits, ground squirrels, and ground chucks. As the group neared a village of domed houses, a chief started to speak in a loud voice; then armed Indians came from the thickets. The speaker was the "poi na'vi,"[52] one of the Pyramid Lake Indian chiefs, who transmitted news of interest to the band.

Frémont found the village to consist of straw huts on higher ground. These houses ("canee") were made of willow and grass and were domed. They were eight to ten feet high with a diameter of eight to fourteen feet. Thatched poles were the frame, then there was a wall, one to two feet thick. There was a smoke hole at the top. The one doorway opened to the east and was flush with the wall. Religion and weather decreed the east opening. The door was made of twined tule, bark, or grass. Mats or layers of grass or tule covered the floor.[53]

Frémont and his party camped on the level bottom lands which were nearly enclosed by the river. The Indians brought large trout ("ai gai") to the whites who were much pleased with the flavor. Frémont knew of the large fish of the Basin Lakes, as Walker had seen and eaten them on his expedition to California. Preuss, in telling about the small river flowing into the lake says, "It teems with the most magnificent salmon trout. For a few farthings, we bought a whole load of them from the Indians. I gorged myself until I almost choked."[54] As Preuss complained continuously about the food throughout the Journey, this was a significant comment. Frémont recorded that the flavor of this trout was superior to that of any fish he had ever known. He compared them with the Columbia River Salmon. They were from two to four feet in length. The Indians may have speared the fish or caught them in nets.[55]

Frémont has left us a vivid description of the natives of the area. He described them as follows:

> ... very fat and (they) appeared to live an easy and happy life. They crowded into the camp more than was consistent with our safety, retaining always their arms, and as they made unsatisfactory demonstrations. they were given to understand that they would not be permitted to come armed into the camp: and strong guards, were kept with the horses ... There is no reason to doubt that these dispositions, uniformly preserved, conducted our party securely through Indians famed for treachery.[56]

The Indians probably knew of other bands having had encounters with the whites, so with armed strangers in their midst they did not discard their bows and arrows. If they had murderous intent they would not have let Frémont record on January 6, "Indians appear to be everywhere prowling like wild animals and there is a fresh trail across the snow in the valley near."[57] Reflecting on Walker's account of the Basin Indians, Frémont was uneasy and ordered vigilant guarding.

He did not know if these Indians had seen whites before but he found some brass buttons and other manifestations of civilization. These may have been obtained from other Paiute or non-Paiute bands who had seen Walker's party, or the fur trappers to the north.[58] Nevertheless, Frémont's party left an indelible impression upon the Indians; for years, the older members told of the howitzer that was carried from Oregon, the only wheeled carriage on this expedition. When there were impassable trails, the gun carriage was taken apart and carried in sections.

As Frémont prepared to leave the lake area, the Indians outlined the lay of the land to the south and southwest for him, and told him how people like himself had crossed the mountains. Frémont did not understand whether they alluded to the Sacramento area or earlier expeditions in the Basin Country. When he asked some of them to guide for a few days on the road, they only looked at each other and smiled. It was January and the Indians declined to attempt crossing the Sierra Nevada at that time of year. Evidently, Frémont contemplated a journey to California before he left the Indians near the mouth of the river.

As the party followed the route of the river, later known as the Truckee, the explorers saw dams made by the Indians for fishing. On the 17th, they left the river. Thus Frémont left the Pyramid Lake area, successful in his explorations and with the realization that Mary's Lake and Buenaventura River were myths.[59]

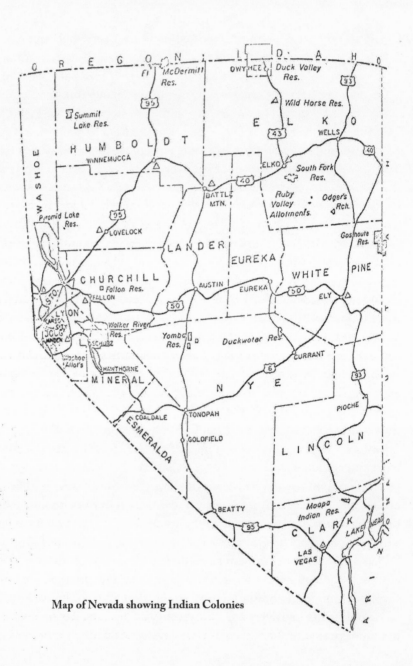

Map of Nevada showing Indian Colonies

CHAPTER V

The Pyramid Lake Wars

As the white men trekked to and from the Pacific Coast across the Neh-muh Tubewah (Northern Paiute area), they created a major obstacle for the Indians, who also were constantly moving from area to area. The territorial and Federal Governments demanded that the Indians move permanently to the reserved lands, but the Neh-muh, who ate meat and vegetables which were obtainable in different areas, could not remain in one region continuously. They were used to moving from one area to another where the plants and animals that formed their diet were plentiful. Hence, when they were forced to remain on the reservation land, their economic balance, as well as their established customs were upset. When the prospectors and miners traversed and settled on prized Neh-muh areas that produced pinenut and other seed plus root foods, specifically in the Virginia City and Como regions, the effect was the same. Furthermore, because the Neh-muh location included parts of the modern states of Nevada, southeastern Oregon, southern Idaho, northeastern and southeastern California, disturbances involving one band affected all the Neh-muh who were closely knit through the various bands.

In the Pyramid Lake Wars of 1860, the Pyramid Lake Indians were forced to retaliate when armed white men invaded their settlement. The underlying causes of these difficulties were grievances of long standing: the encroachment of white men on their prized lands along the Truckee River and in the Como and Virginia City regions, promiscuous killings of Indians in the Humboldt River area; and the killing of game and waste of native food by the whites. In simple terms, the entrance of the white man into the domain of the Nevada Indians had disrupted the Indian economy and their societal structure, but provided no substitute in return. Under those circumstances, antagonism between the two groups was inevitable.

The Indians did not plan the Pyramid Lake Wars, having always been a peaceable people.[60] Although they early developed legitimate grievances against white men, they had wished for a parley with some of the respected whites, with the hope that they could reach equitable adjustments. Nevertheless, their awareness of some of their limitations, principally their lack of fluency in the English language, led them to refuse any meeting with whites similar to the parley held by Winnemucca around January 28, 1860. And on the other hand, these grievances were disregarded by the white officials and citizens.

The Pyramid Lake Wars were triggered by the whites.[61] Suspicions and hysteria generated by the Williams Station killing by Indians; greed for the Indian's best farm lands, and for the lands which possibly contained rich minerals; total disregard of human dignity and life; and a traditional lack of respect for the Indians military capacity—all these factors promoted an atmosphere that led to the outbreak of war. Specific preliminaries to the Pyramid Lake wars included suspicions of Indian activities at Pyramid Lake, the greed and hysteria of Roop County and Virginia City, and the Carson River men's abuse of Indian women. By the beginning of 1859, the stage was set for a serious conflict.

On January 4, 1859, Agent Dodge said there were about 1,705 Paiutes congregated adjacent to Pyramid Lake,[62] divided into six groups. Most of them were visiting bands who had come to catch the salmon trout which were starting up the Truckee River to spawn at this time of the year. Old Winnemucca's band consisted of 155 members, and Young Winnemucca's about 300.[63] While at Pyramid Lake the bands met socially with the local groups. After the fishing and preservation of the catch, there was visiting, dancing, gaming, and a generally happy time. Although this was a customary gathering, it created fear among the white men; for the next year when a similar gathering of Paiute bands was in the same location the whites erroneously considered it a war council.[64]

When Peter Lassen was killed in Black Rock Range northeast of Gerlach, the Paiutes from Winnemucca's band were blamed (this area is now known as Clapper's Canyon). "Provision" Governor Roop appointed commissioners to get the culprits. On January 28, 1860, the commission left for the Paiute camp, but finding it deserted, they went on to Pyramid Lake. There they found Old Winnemucca, who refused to take part in the return of any Indians to Honey Lake. The Honey Lake area was the locale of Winnemucca's band. He had bargained for $1,600 for the Honey Lake Valley and one to two beef each week from the stockmen of the region, but the whites refused to bargain. He figured if the white men were to take his band area they should pay for it.[65]

At the time of the Pyramid Lake Wars, Major Dodge was the agent of the Indians, and when he was absent, Major W. H. H. Wasson was the acting agent. The Indians had written to the agent's office telling of the game, and the destruction of the pinenut trees.[66] The Kuyui Dokado's pinenut region was the Virginia City and Como areas, where rich mineral lands had been opened by the whites.

In 1860 the leader of the Kuyui Dokado band was Numaga. He had lived among the whites in California, and spoke fluent English. He realized the superiority of the white men in implements of warfare and thus was opposed to any conflicts with them. He was an intelligent, eloquent, and courageous leader. He had several successful conferences with the whites.[67]

The immediate events leading to the first Pyramid Lake War began with the murders committed on May 7, 1860, at Williams Station, situated on a knoll east of the big bend on the Carson River, for which the Indians were blamed.[68] Some of the white pioneers living in the Neh-muh country did not have high morals. They had no respect for the Indian women, and were much disliked by the Indians for this disregard. Inevitably trouble arose, because the Neh-muh always held their women in high regard and respect, they refused to condone the mistreatment of them by anyone Indian or Caucasian. Indian women were held captives at Williams Station, and the belief was that Indian men murdered the whites at the station and released the women. Frederick Dodge, the Indian Agent, reported that "Two intruders on the reserve and their gross outrages on Indian women lie one great cause of the present troubles."[69] When the news of the murders reached Virginia City, the whites appealed for volunteers to punish the accused and received an immediate response, so that hastily formed detachments of poorly armed, undisciplined, and inexperienced men were raised.[70] This hysteria led to an invasion of an Indian camp and the killing of many whites and Indians.[71]

On May 12, five days after the murders at Williams Station, the white invaders first saw the Indians on high land in a thicket of tall brush.[72] The Indians had three large camps along the foot of the bench land near the site of the 1924 trading post at Nixon, NV. They climbed that bench to watch the approaching whites. It was then the whites saw them.[73]

The whites assembled about one hundred men. An Indian on a horse advanced toward the group waving a white flag. Suddenly A. B. Elliot fired on the one warrior with the periscope rifle. It was then Major Ormsby ordered the men to charge. About thirty men responded, while the others panicked; the Indians ran for cover. Observing that the horses ridden by the whites were tired, the Indians closed in and almost surrounded the whites

A reporter for the *Daily Alta California* of May 20, 1860 stated "The previous conduct of the Indians, as far as I have been able to learn, would indicate that they had no desire to war with the settlements in this vicinity."[74]

In 1924, Johnny Calico, a Paiute Indian who was twelve years old when the Pyramid Lake Wars were fought related incidents of the war through his son, Fred, who spoke fluent English and Paiute.[75] He said that at the firing of the whites' guns, the Indians ran for cover. Many white men ran back to the old trail over which they had come. Then Chiquita (Young) Winnemucca chased them while Indians along the trail shot at the fleeing whites. After the white men reached the trail where a hill came down to the river, only four or five small Indian parties followed. He said Ormsby, being wounded, offered the Indians his powder cans and pistol, while begging for his life, but another Indian from the rear shot him. From that point, the Indians returned to their camp. He did not know how many whites had been killed, but said no Indians were killed, however, three were wounded.

Many details of Calico's statements were the same as those of Captain R.G. Watkins, who was in the battle and who described it. The place of Ormsby's death as indicated by Calico was probably correct as the Indians had pointed to it in many discussions. Furthermore, this battle was misnamed because it was actually fought about four miles from the lake.

Both Indians and whites were surprised at the outcome of the first Pyramid Lake War. The Indians were surprised that the whites had put up such a poor showing with the number of men that they had. The whites were surprised that the Indians had not easily been beaten. The whites, reflecting on the battle, vowed retaliation and planned a second offensive.

A citizen expressed the view of many white residents of Nevada Territory when he wrote from Virginia City on May 14, 1860, denouncing the band. He argued that the whites needed more troops from the other side of the Sierra, because the next war was to be one "of extermination." In his view, there were a half dozen or more tribes united to whip the whites "again and again."[76]

Even then, en route for the retaliatory assault on the Pyramid Lake Indians were numerous military units. On Tuesday, May 15, 1860, General Haven and Colonel Tozier passed through Placerville, California, to the Nevada Territory, with an escort of men and 500 stands of arms and 100,000 rounds of ammunition. On the evening of the same date, Captain Stewart and his aide, Flint, arrived with 150 regular soldiers and 30,000 rounds of ammunition, and they made arrangements for a company to haul the troops to Carson Valley, then left the next day. Lieutenant Gibson, with ten men and two howitzers, reached Placerville on Thursday. They hoped to catch up with Captain Stewart before he reached Virginia City.[77]

When the cavalry from Honey Lake met the volunteers and regular army from California at the big bend of the Truckee River, scouts reported that 100 Indians were approaching. On June 2, 1860, the second battle of Pyramid Lake was fought. A three-hour battle ensued; the Indians fled at dusk after a loss of approximately 160 men. Two whites were killed and two or three were wounded; the main force followed the Indians and subdued them.[78]

After the wars, Major W. H. H. Wasson, acting agent, listened to the Indians' account of the war through an interpreter, George Crip. The Indians gesticulated, and many times they did not know the answers to his questions. They located places of death struggles for him.[79]

After the Pyramid Lake Wars, leaders of the attack on the Indians had time to think over and assess the wars. They remembered the Indians were few in number, and had frail ponies, were poorly armed, and had been friendly despite previous provocation. Finally, only a few had revenged the abuse of certain Indian women, and some recognized even that perhaps the Williams Station depredation was not the work of the Indians at all. In short, some regretted their haste in invading the Indian reservation.[80] Nevertheless, there remained many causes of friction between the Indians and the white pioneers, between the Indians and the Indian Administration, and between them and their leader Numaga. For example, when the whites demanded of Numaga that he keep his Indians near the lake, the Indians felt restricted and they turned bitter words against him. Understandably, they mocked his display of friendliness to the whites, who had recently invaded the sanctuary promised for the Indians by the Territorial Government. They also readily concluded that the whites, when demanding their band areas for the Indian reservation at Pyramid Lake, were insincere.

The legacy of these conflicts also included other issues. As the Kuyui Dokado had experienced the wrath of the soldiers, stories concerning the brutality of white soldiers survived as a living reality. Conversely, the Indians were distrusted by the white soldiers, though among their greatest white friends and leaders would be reckoned Major Dodge and Major Wasson. Furthermore, because of their restriction to the reservation area, the Indians were hampered in their pursuit of agricultural activities vital to their survival. Eventually their frustration was aggravated because of poor farming equipment and improper irrigation facilities. Utter lack of water, and the loss of the best farm lands to trespassers and the coming of the railroad later added to their frustration. When urged to remain close to the lake, they did, but they clearly felt that the restriction was too severe: they were dependent upon access to different areas where they could secure various foods. If the Paiute bands traveled as they had before the arrival of the whites, they were classed as dangerous to the pioneer routes. Accordingly, some were forced to reservations in Oregon and Washington, where they were very unhappy with the change in environment.

If the Paiutes had not been a highly disciplined people from their culture, they might have constituted a dangerous threat to the pioneers traveling on the nation's central route to California by wagon and rail, to the Pony Express route, to the telegraph system, and to the white settlements. Instead, they realized the ultimate futility of war with the whites, and tried to integrate themselves with the white culture.

CHAPTER VI

Federal Legislation Pertaining to the Pyramid Lake Indians

Governmental Indian policies, both British and American, have been varied. Indeed, few consistent policies were ever developed. During Colonial days, the English Crown and the Colonies had regulated trade between their subjects and the Indians but had originally made no attempt to govern the Indian tribes. After the French and Indian wars, however, Britain created two Superintendencies of Indian Affairs, one for the northern and one for the southern colonies, to promote trade and to keep peace between the Indians and the border settlers. Under the threat of war, the Continental Congress on July 12, 1775, asserted jurisdiction over Indian tribes and created three Departments of Indian Affairs, marking the beginning of United States Indian policy. Commissioners headed the three departments and their duties were to preserve peace and friendship, and to prevent Indians from aiding the British forces in the War for Independence. The Spanish policy of founding the missions for Indians with the aid of the conquistadors and settlers from 1776 to the end of its dominion in 1822 was a way of settlement and rule in the Indian territory.

The first Congress under the Federal Constitution on August 7, 1789, subsequently established the War Department, and all direction of Indian Affairs was entrusted to its Secretary. Under his jurisdiction, trading houses were maintained from 1796 to 1822. These houses supplied the Indians with goods at fair prices and offered a fair price for furs in exchange. The Indian agents were appointed by the President and were responsible to him: all accounts were transmitted through the Secretary of the Treasury. The office of Superintendent of Indian Trade, an experiment in administration of Indian affairs, was set up in 1806 and abolished in 1822.

Twenty years before Frémont met Pyramid Lake Indians, the Federal Bureau of Indian Affairs was created by the Secretary of War, John C. Calhoun.[81] The Bureau created only confusion for eight years, 1824 to 1832. During this time the Indians saw their tribal areas being occupied by ever increasing numbers of whites, and they became belligerent. Many Indian tribes from the East were removed to territory beyond the Mississippi River, so that their home lands might be used by the white settlers. Although the War Department supervised the removals, a change in Federal policy was already in progress. On July 9, 1832,[82] a Commissioner of Indian Affairs was appointed, and by 1834, the Bureau was predominantly controlled by civilians. However, not until March 3, 1849, was the Bureau transferred from the War Department to the newly established Department of the Interior.[83]

Between 1824 and 1850 the government began to confine Indians to restricted areas. However, they became frustrated when they were forced together on a reservation and also when moved from place to place. The governmental policy from 1851-1868 was expanded to encourage Indians to become independent and useful citizens. Recommendations were made that Indians be granted United States citizenship. This constituted a different approach from those of removal and segregation. Individual ownership of land was beginning to be recognized as one way of helping progress toward citizenship. The Indians did not always use the large tracts of land set aside for reservations, nor did they understand the meaning of individual property ownership. Seeming Indian indolence and the white traders' fraudulent practices on the Indian reservations were recognized by officials of the National Administration. Consequently, the traders were required to be licensed and improved agricultural implements and substantial garments were requested for the Indian instead of blankets, trinkets, and bright colored cloths.

From 1868-1877, the reservation Indians were controlled by agents chosen by a new system as follows: under President Grant, nominations of agents were delegated to various religious bodies which were active in missionary work. Other agencies were filled by army officers until the Appropriation Act of July 15, 1870, which obliged them to relinquish their civil posts. Treaty making was abandoned on March 3, 1871, because the Indians were beginning to assume a national independence.[84]

Legislation from 1880-1890 attempted to assimilate the Indians into the white culture, thus launching a new era of Indian-white man relations in the United States. The most important piece of legislation was the "Allotment" or Dawes Act of February 8, 1887, which reorganized some previous practices concerning Indians and their reservation lands. The Allotment system was intended to protect the Indians' interests, and to prepare them to handle their own affairs as independent members of society. The Act authorized the President to allot reservation lands to the tribal Indians who were living there. The head of the Indian family was allowed to choose land for his allotment, if he had improved a particular piece of land previously. He was to be given 160 acres and 40 to 60 acres additional for each child. The allotment was held in trusteeship by the President of the United States until such time as the Indian had proved himself capable of owning the land, when he could receive a fee patent. Otherwise the President would continue his guardianship. After each Indian resident was given an allotment, the remaining lands were sold, and the proceeds were held by the United States Treasury for Congressional appropriation for the education of the tribe. The Act gave preference to Indians who wished to work in the Indian Service. This Act was passed in 1887, at the time of the great migration of settlers to the West,[85] when the frontier was rapidly disappearing. The whites desired Indian reserved lands which were not utilized by the Indians. Many people surmised the Indians would never use all the reserved land, especially when they integrated into the white culture.

Another important piece of Indian legislation passed on June 2, 1924,[86] was an Act which authorized citizenship to all American Indians residing in the jurisdiction of the United States. The passage of this Act was accomplished by the aid of the American Legion and other interested groups. Indian youths had volunteered and served in World War I, even though legally they were not citizens of the United States. This Act gave the Pyramid Lake Indians a new impetus to their lives. They learned the requisites for voting, and, with the help of their leaders and Indian Service personnel, they exercised their suffrage prerogative.

Another area of Federal legislation dealt with education, medicine, agricultural assistance, and social welfare. In 1934, the states were given authority to provide aid to Indians in those fields.[87] Contracts were to be made so that Congress would appropriate money for this care and turn the money over to the State. The Indian Service facilities could be used. The services to the Indians were to be the highest that the states could provide. The Secretary of the Interior was to report annually to Congress on the progress of the activities specified in this contract.

In 1953, Federal school property located on the reservation not to exceed twenty acres, could be transferred to the local public school districts or public agencies. The property was available to both Indian and non-Indian children. The mineral deposits were reserved by the United States. This land can revert to the United States. Following this Act, the Federal Indian School property at Nixon was transferred to the Public Schools of Nevada.[88]

Another Act of August 27, 1935, was for promoting education in crafts and business for adults and children. An Indian Arts and Crafts Board was created.[89] The Nevada Indians set up the "Wa-Pai-Shone Craftsmen, Incorporation" with the aid of Federal employees at Stewart, Nevada. The tribes sold their wares of basketry, beaded ornaments, buckskin clothing, bows and arrows, and Indian souvenirs. Later the location was moved to Nixon, Nevada, where the Wa-Pai-Shone Craftsmen, Incorporated, is still in operation.

Indian legislation from 1930-1940 was notable. During that period Indians were relieved of great costs imposed upon them by the government as explained later, for reimbursable projects, although some of these projects were not requested by Indians and some gave little benefit. Then the comprehensive act of June 18 1934, (Wheeler-Howard) prohibited further allotment of reservation lands, because many Indians had sold their allotted lands. The Indians were allowed to govern many of their affairs on the reservations through the tribal councils with supervision from the Federal Government. They could borrow money to buy necessary equipment and supplies. The Indians were allowed to accept or decline the provisions of the Act.

The Federal policy of Indian land allotment was reversed when the Indian tribes ratified the Reorganization Act of 1934.[90] The Pyramid Lake group accepted the terms of this law, which also was known as the Indian New Deal. By this law, a revolving fund was established to make loans for economic development; Sections 16 and 17 permitted tribal organization with a constitution and by-law which were to be ratified by a majority vote. The tribal council ruled over the affairs of the reservation with the aid of the Federal Agency superintendent. The council could employ legal counsel, but the choice of the lawyer and the fixing of fees were to be with the approval of the Secretary of the Interior. The tribal council could prevent the sale, lease, and disposition of tribal lands. It could negotiate with the Federal and State and local governments. It could receive information concerning all appropriations and estimates of projects for the tribe's benefit in preparation for the submission of annual estimates to the Bureau of the Budget and Congress.

Many early Federal laws and most of the Indian treaties have now only historical value. Today, Indian policy is generally established by special legislation.[91]

Turning back in time over 100 years, we see that after gold was found in California in 1848, the main overland route traveled by the emigrants pierced the territory of the Nevada Indians; some clashes occurred when the pioneers began to settle in Nevada. Treaty making by the government with Indians was on the decline, so the Paiutes of Nevada had no treaty. The Federal policy of moving Indians to reserves was in practice at this time, so the Paiutes of

Nevada were ordered to reservations. Continued clashes between Indians and emigrants finally forced legislation to control the trouble.

On January 4, 1859, Major Frederick Dodge, the Indian agent at Carson Valley, Utah Territory, requested an Indian reserve to prevent Indians from encountering the pioneers, and to provide security for Indians whose hunting grounds were being traversed by whites.[92]

In seeking an asylum for the Nevada Indians, Dodge lamented the depredations against Indians of the "Wa Sho," "Pah Ute," and Shoshone tribes under his jurisdiction. He felt that the (white) moral atmosphere surrounding the Indians was unhealthy. He asked for one large reserve for both the "Pah Utes" and "Wa Shos", requesting that the Truckee River Valley (Truckee Meadows), which is the present site of Reno, be retained for that purpose.

Though deploring the general conditions of Nevada Indians, Dodge also showed sympathy with them. He said:

> The Pah Utes are undoubtly the most interesting and docile Indi-
> ans on the continent. By proper management, these Indians may
> be made to compete with the whites in agricultural pursuits. They
> are extremely anxious to cultivate their lands and will make excel-
> lent men to work. They have never received any presents from the
> government, or from any government officers until now, except a
> few things given them by Dr. Hurt some two or three years ago.[93]

Interesting and docile the Pah Utes may have been, but in 1859 there were conflicts between the Indians and the pioneers, in the Sublette Cutoff in Oregon, Mr. J. Forney, Superintendent of Indian Affairs, Utah Territory, dispatched the military to the area on this occasion to quell the raiding Indians. Sometimes families were shot by the white soldiers.[94]

After these army and Indian conflicts, Agent Dodge, on November 25, 1859, requested the Commissioner of Indian Affairs to establish a reservation at Pyramid Lake for the Pah Utes and "other Indians."[95] His reference to the "other Indians" may have been to the remnants of Indians in the Oregon battles. He was not sure they were Paiutes. On December 8, 1859, the Commissioner of the General Land Office wrote to the surveyor general in Salt Lake City, ordering him to reserve the Pyramid Lake Tract of land mapped and described by Agent Dodge, for the Indians. However, it was to be fifteen years before the Pyramid lake area was officially proclaimed an Indian reservation.

Between 1861 and 1864, Territorial Governor James W. Nye made some efforts to improve relations between the Indians and the whites. In 1861 he and

Agent W. H. Wasson met with some Indian leaders at Camp Stoney, 40 miles from Fort Churchill. At the meeting, the Governor emphasized the necessity for cooperation from the Indians in the territory. He explained Federal projects such as the overland stage route and the new telegraph system. He emphasized the protection United States citizens receive from their government, particularly of their property, and asserted that this protection also extended to the Indians and their property.[96]

Though a Federal survey conducted by Eugene Monroe was not formally made for the territorial reserve of the Pyramid Lake Indian site until 1865, the Indians accepted Governor Nye's explanation and subsequently assumed they were being protected by the Federal government.[97] However, there were anxious days and years when the Indians saw pioneers settling on the posted areas of the proposed reservation. It was not until March 23, 1874, that President Ulysses Simpson Grant officially proclaimed the Pyramid Lake Indian reserve. Agent Bateman was elated at the executive order which set aside 640,815 acres of land for the Indians, and he asserted that President Grant would be remembered as a "true friend of the Indians."[98] The nearest military post, located at the Presidio, California, was offered as assurance that the military forces were available in case of conflict between whites and Indians.[99]

After an interval of fifteen years following the Federal allotment plan, the Reclamation Act of June 17, 1902, permitted the land disposal of the Pyramid Lake Reservation in Nevada. The Secretary of the Interior was authorized to "reclaim, utilize, and dispose of the lands in said reservation as though the same were a part of the Public Domain,"[100] except there must be five acres of irrigable lands allotted to each Indian on the reservation. The remainder of the irrigable lands were to be allowed settlers who would pay added charges per acre to the value of the unallotted land before reclamation. That chargeable amount was to be determined by the Secretary of the Interior. Part of the proceeds would be the payment for the reclamation, and under the Secretary's direction the rest would revert to the tribe. The Act was never enforced, because of the presence of the white squatters on the reservation and because not enough land was available.

In 1916, Congress appropriated $30,000 to improve, enlarge, and extend the irrigation system to 3,300 acres of land in the Pyramid Lake Reservation.[101] The total expenditure was not to exceed $85,000. The next year $30,000 more was appropriated,[102] and finally $25,000 in 1918.[103] The government was to be reimbursed by the tribe. Previously small amounts had been appropriated for irrigation ditches. The Indians prepared and kept the ditches without technical advise; therefore, the ditches weren't efficient.

Federal legislation was continued to solve the Pyramid Lake Reservation problems of the entrymen on its land, and its water rights to the Truckee River.

Chief of Police – Captain Dave, Pyramid Lake
Courtesy of Harry Huston

CHAPTER VII

The Entrymen in the Reservation

At the bend of the Coo-yu-e Hoop (Coo-yu-e River) the verdant land and the fresh water river teeming with fish tempted the pioneers to remain. Several families made homes in this part of the Reserve, but when told they were trespassing most of them moved away.

Through many successive years, the Pyramid Lake Indians lost their best agricultural lands to trespassers on the reserve. "Squatting" by the whites on the reservation started soon after the land was set aside by the territorial government. In 1850, Agent Dodge posted notice that certain areas of the Truckee River and areas all around Pyramid Lake were forbidden to citizens of Utah Territory, but whites disregarded it. In May 1866, the Superintendent of Indian Affairs in Nevada reminded the Commissioner of his letter dated March 28, which stated that four white men were intruding on the reservation.[104] He had asked them to leave, but they refused. He communicated with Lieutenant Colonel A.E. Hooker, then commander of the District of Nevada, who delegated eight soldiers to eject the squatters by force should it be necessary. The soldiers and the agent met and went to the residence of the squatters. Seeing the soldiers, the squatters left.

Captain Dave, the police chief, and his son, Robert A. Davidson, made a map of Pyramid Lake and its surrounding area in 1885.[105] The Indians understood the reservation boundary was "from peak to peak;" there being no fences to show the exact boundary line. Consequently, when the Indians saw other people using the land and water for farming and fishing, they wondered if those people were not trespassers on the reserve. This map with the Neh-muh names indicates the lakes, rivers, mountains, and farm lands of the Indians and Caucasian entrymen as of the time.

Coo-yu-ee Pah (Panunadu) is the lake. Az Go Yuir was the Indian name for Winnemucca Lake; interpreted it means gray ku yui. The mountain between the two lakes is Pa du guar meaning "between." In this ridge were the caves (taws) where some of the people lived. Sometimes it was called "Nah a quin" (shot at) for the time of the Second Pyramid Lake battle, 1860, when most of the women, children, and the aged took refuge in the caves.

Pa van car te di is Anaho Island.

To the north are the needles of Pi da wa you ar. Here is the legendary domain of the water babies. In this area three Caucasians had ranches on the reservation. The captain understandably asked who had given them permission to trespass. Wiar car ter ter is Juniper Mountain, Limbo point was called Yun ga nee (mountain of small shrubs).

To the northwest is Big Mountain, Par bar gar ter ter, which was good for stock and ranching.

To the south is Te mo hav in Mountain, interpreted the "Lookout." General comment was that again this area was good for ranching. The Captain inquired if the Caucasian sheepmen grazing sheep there were on the reservation legally. Sar yar da ka in was the site of the hunters' village for the mudhen (coot), a staple part of the diet. In the fall the mudhens were fat and plentiful. The families congregated to hunt and dry the winter's supply of these birds, simultaneously feasting, dancing, and visiting.

To the southeast, the Chinese had been fishing in the Az Go Yuir (Gray Ku Yui) lake. The sites were recorded on the map. The Chinese were allowed to sell their fish whereas the Indians were granted no permits; consequently the latter were puzzled by this injustice. Also in this area Mr. Wheeler had a sheep camp each year which indicated trespassing.

The Coo-yu-ee Lake was twenty-two miles from Wadsworth, the railroad town. From the reservation house to Az Go Yuir Lake was eight miles.

Several miles to the east were the Twin Peaks or Wah ho Coda Yuir Gar u, where there was good grazing for the horses.

Near the mouth of the river was located the natural amphitheater where the horse races and Indian games were held.

Indians who held designated farm lands were:

Bumper George	---Jim
Bumper George's father	---Jim
Bob Holbrook	Mack Jones
George Holbrook	Washoe Jimmy
Jim Swain	Jimmy ----
----Johnson	Winnemucca Charley
Rawhide Henry	

Designated here was the reservation house:

Smith	Tom King
George Queep	Old Hickory
Truckee Pete	----
----Bronco	---- Frank
Calico Johnny	Robert Frank
Whiskey Ben	Mat Winnemucca
George Holbrook	Joe Jim
B----	Young Tom
Harry----	Big Joe
Tom Lee	Big Mouth
Jeff Davis	

To the south:

Winnemucca Natche	Captain Sam (Near Reservation Dam)
Charley Winnemucca	

The Kuyui Dokado each had an Indian name given especially to the individual, but after the integration with the whites they began using English names, to simplify their identity. They chose names at random or those of their employers.

The map shows the townsite of Wadsworth and the Central Pacific Railroad.

At this time Caucasian farmers on the reservation were Bob Gochen, Old Gochen, John Lee, R. Hill, Jake Hamilton, Joe ----, and Oldenhouse.

It was not until the late 1930's when Miss Alida Bowler was Superintendent of the Nevada Indian Agency that the Pyramid Lake Reservation was surveyed and fenced. The Indians were astounded to find their "peak to peak" boundary was just legendary and the size of their reserve greatly depleted.

Later Indian Service officials did not use militia or civil police to evict the squatters on the reservation, so other whites came to reside on the lands reserved for Paiutes in the Pyramid Lake and the Truckee River areas. In 1912, the Federal Map, Number 6788 Tube Number 780, showed that Edward J. Posvar and John Garavanta were farming Indian lands south and southwest of the Wadsworth townsite. William H. Pearson was using Neh-muh Tubewah east and south at the turn of the river. To the north and east of the town Elias Olinghouse held four tracts of land. Down the river Domenico Ceresola, J.B. Sturla and Company, Joseph

Gardella and Thomas H Blundell were entrymen on the Pyramid Lake Indian Reservation.

Then by the Act of June 7, 1924, these people were permitted to purchase the land upon which they had been twenty-one years or longer at a cash price of $1.25 per acre or at a rate set by the Secretary of the Interior.[106] No more than 640 acres were to be sold to a person or a corporation. Lots in the townsite of Wadsworth were to be surveyed and sold. The sale of the land was to be made through the local land office within ninety days; then if payment was not made, the United States would make entry and take possession of the lands for the Paiute Indians of Pyramid Lake Indian Reservation. In Section 3, the entrymen with patents were recognized. Legally the Indians began to lose the best of their agricultural land.

James Shaw, an Indian, expressed the sentiment of the Kuyui Dokado after a meeting at the Wadsworth government school building:

> If the white settlers upon our reservation should not pay for the land they have squated (Sic) upon ... at the expiration of the 90 days agreed upon, they should be removed therefrom. We made a mistake in allowing (them) ever to settle upon our lands. The Indians want our lands so they can make a home for themselves.[107]

When he said that they allowed the settlement, he did not mean there was a formal allowance. The Indians relied on the Federal Government to protect their land so they had made no move to keep the whites from settling on the reservation. The Indians remembered the agreement on cooperation between the governments of the Territory of the United States and the Indians for governmental protection. Had the Indians not been so naive they would have protested in writing to the Federal officials, and would have persuaded their white friends to do likewise.

On May 21, 1934, there were still eight entrymen who had not paid for the reservation lands on which they were living, and an act of Congress extended the time for their payment.[108] Senate Bill, 1776, (April 23, 1935), was a continuation of the similar bill of 1934.

The tribal council then wrote letters to the Nevada Congressmen quoting the amount owed the Indians by the entrymen. The land appraisal was $44,336.92. First payment on the principal, $11,135.76, was made on June 8, 1925. The buyers protested and did not pay the interest of 5% or the remainder of the principal. The tribe estimated $1,660 was owed per year as simple interest. The council stated that:

They (entrymen) cannot possibly need this money more than do the people of this reservation. We are very poor. But we are anxious to work hard to use our land and other resources so that all of our people may have a decent living and be self-supporting . . . If we cannot have the money then we feel that the land should become ours again, and its products would help us to have better living conditions.[109]

There were continuous legal conflicts over this land. In the United States District Court for the District of Nevada, the opinion and decision of Judge Norcross was to give patents for the reservation land to the whites.[110] Eventually, the case was taken to the US Circuit Court of Appeals for the 9th Circuit in San Francisco, where the first decision was reversed.[111] One defendant took his case to the United States Supreme Court which refused the writ of a certiorari. So in 1944, the 300 acres of unsold land near Wadsworth was restored to the Indians. Because of these various delays Congress permitted the entrymen twenty years to buy the choice farm lands of the reservation instead of the ninety days as first specified in the Act of June 7, 1924.

Even after this, Senator McCarran in 1943 introduced and supported several bills to give the land to the white claimants.[112] The Indians and their friends had to be aware of those bills to see that they did not pass Congress. Senate Bill 24 was one of these bills. Indian Service officials in Washington asked in the Committee hearings that no bills similar to S. 24 be considered, as the courts had made decisions favoring the Indians, and the Pyramid Lake Indians needed security to use the lands that were rightfully theirs. The Indians, being organized under the Indian Reorganization Act of 1934, could prevent sale of land according to Section 16.[113]

The law of 1934, the Reorganization Act, was disregarded by the claimants, their lawyers, and some congressmen when they insisted that Pyramid Lake Indian Reservation lands be given to the white "squatters."

When the legality of the Indian Reservation was proved, the water rights were also established. These rights were the first on the Truckee River. The final decree was made by US District Judge Frank H. Norcross on September 8, 1944.[114]

Finally on November 1, 1951, Mr. Dillon Myers, Commissioner of Indian Affairs, authorized the Justice Department to serve the whites notice of trespass on the Pyramid Lake Reservation.[115] The Indians were disheartened because the best agricultural lands of the reservation were given to the entrymen. The disputed lands returned to the Indians were not as good as those given to the entrymen.

On August 13, 1946, an Indian Claims Commission was created and established.[116] This Act allowed the tribes who had no formal treaties with the United States to make claims against the government which had taken their areas from them without compensation. Using this act as the basis, the Northern Paiute presented their land claims in 1950.

When the Paiutes filed their claim, tribal members testified at the Claims hearing, held in Reno, January 1951. Legends and personal experiences were related as evidence for establishment of tribal control of the Nevada lands before the arrival of the whites.

The Commission was to decide whether the whites took this land and determine its value. It divided the Northern Paiutes into four groups, and established their territory, leaving strips between the four areas to which specific groups would be designated when more evidence was received. The land value would be estimated as of a date set by negotiation or a later decision from briefs given to the Claims Commission.

In 1959, the Paiute bands were recognized as controllers of Nevada lands prior to the coming of the whites. This was a preliminary decision of the Indian Claims Commission in Washington, D.C.[117]

The Pyramid Lake Indians, as a whole, abide by all the statutes set up for them, and they have been patient when others were not. Those Indians who were left on the reserve were pleased when the land around the lake was set aside for them as they felt secure from the white pioneers and soldiers. When the best agricultural lands of the reservation were legally transferred to the "squatters," the Indians were very discouraged. The older ones encouraged the young to get an education so as to work and live as the state society demanded. However, they chose to stay on the reservation and live as before. Later, even though living conditions were poor and meager, that reservation meant home for the ones who chose to remain, while others sought livelihood elsewhere.

CHAPTER VIII

Economic Development 1859-1959

The original native economy was sufficient for the support of the Kuyui Dokado at the time of Frémont's arrival in the Basin area. As other Paiute bands were placed on the Pyramid Lake Reservation, however, a shortage of plant and large animal food troubled the Indians, and the government gradually became involved in the economic problems.

The economic development of the Pyramid Lake Reservation was hampered by the continual change of agents, unreliable water flow into the lake, squatters who encroached upon the land and helped to deplete the supply of fish, and insufficient government appropriations. Although most of the Indian agents considered the Paiutes industrious, the Indians were troubled by repeated agricultural failures. For this reason many Indians eventually migrated into the white settlements to seek work. The passage of the Central Pacific Railroad through the reservation gave the Indians the opportunity to work in the railroad town of Wadsworth.

Constant change of agents was not beneficial to the Indians for it created insecurity among people who needed dedicated agents to promote the fusion of the native and white cultures. Though most of the agents were interested in the Paiutes, political influence, tardy and insufficient appropriations, isolation, and personal greed gave impetus to haphazard leadership. Furthermore, inequality in fishing rights and poor fishing procedures delayed sound economic development of the area.

Fishery
Though Julian H. Steward classed most of the Northern Paiutes as seed-gatherers and hunters,[118] the Kuyui Dokado Band name indicated the people were fishermen too. Frederick Dodge, the first Pyramid Lake agent, said that near the "Coo-you-e-hoop" (Kuyui River), or the Salmon River, an excellent fishery could be maintained.[119]

1870-80 trout sold for 5¢ per pound, Wadsworth, Nevada.
Courtesy of Harry Huston

The importance of fish in the Indians' diet was mentioned in many reports. Farming on the Truckee River Reservation was unsuccessful because of the scarcity of water,[120] and Governor Nye noted that the shortage of rain and snow in the area would give lesser yield of natural seeds, roots, and pinenuts, and with the absence of much vegetable food the Indians would need to dry more fish for the winter and spring diet. While some Paiute bands of the state suffered in the two-year drought (1871-72), the Pyramid Lake band was not hungry, because of an adequate fish supply.[121] The next year (1873) the Indians sold to the white settlers the surplus fish that was not needed for their food.[122]

Trespassing by white fishermen was constantly reported. On July 15, 1879, for instance, some white trespassers were found guilty in the Federal Court at Carson City.[123] Their appeal was heard in the United States Circuit Court in November 1879, and the lower court ruling was reaffirmed. The trespassers, who were to have been sentenced on December 1, 1879, did not report, for they knew they had many white sympathizers, and they disregarded the Federal court order. Agent James E. Spencer reported that everything was in poor condition and "trespassers were running riot on fields and fisheries."[128] The whites wanted to be allowed to fish on the reservation, but the agent said the fishery was more valuable to the Indians than farming, if it could be kept from the trespassers. In 1885, a trespassing fisherman, Sherman, was jailed, so there was no more trouble that year with white trespassers at the fishery. Meanwhile, the Chinese, who had worked on the Central Pacific Railroad,

Jim Erb And Harry Huston (1880-1890) sold fish to Dick Cowles for $.05 per pound.
Courtesy of Harry Huston

Cutthroat Trout, 20 Pounds, 1929, caught by Willie Smith and James Calvin, Nixon, Nevada

were getting fish at Mud Lake (or Winnemucca Lake) and were selling the fish. The Indians protested, because they believed the lake was theirs.[125]

In the early years of the reservation period, fishing was profitable.[126] In 1883, 75,000 pounds of fish sold at seven cents per pound, and grossed $5,250.[127] This was for the actual sale to outside parties. In 1885, Agent Gibson told of fish selling for $5,000.[128] He reported other instances of profitable sales. In 1886, fish sales netted $5,000;[129] In 1888, $3,600.[130] Fish brought more cash to the Indians than did any other product, but in 1895, Agent I.S. Wootten said the fish revenue had declined steadily.[131]

The Indians tried to implement their dwindling cash returns by renting boats from white settlers for fishing on the lake, but this proved unprofitable, because the whites marketed the fish for the Indians, who were paid whatever the whites desired after the rentals were deducted. Therefore Agent Spriggs requested more boats for the Indians and the building of a wharf for their use.[132] But even with boats, income from fishing declined still further because of low water in the Truckee River, brought about largely by the construction of dams to benefit white ranchers and the urban areas of Reno and Sparks.

On May 20, 1943, at the hearing before the committee on Indian Affairs of the House of Representatives, pertaining to Senate Bill 24, the chairman of the Pyramid Lake Tribal Council was asked if the Indians could fish for a living, and he answered negatively, because the Pyramid Lake fish had been practically

Curtis Harnar, 1958, showing two Coo-Yu-ee he caught in the Coo-Yu-ee-Pah (Pyramid Lake).

exterminated.[133] The salmon trout and the kuyui could not spawn in the Truckee River, because of the low water level and the impossibility of passage over the dams. Though a fish ladder had been added to the Numana Dam on the reservation near Nixon, there never was enough water for the fish to clear it.

When the Nevada Fish and Game Department began planting the cutthroat trout in the lake, the tribal average yearly income for 1956 and 1957 was $7,377. This money went into the Tribal Fund, from which Tribal projects were maintained. Most of this amount was received from fishing permits sold to people other than tribal members.[134]

Agriculture

When the reservation period began, the Kuyui Dokado continued some of their ancient methods of getting a livelihood, but they were given opportunity to learn to farm as that they they had practiced agriculture before. Agent Dodge reported that they were anxious to learn how to cultivate their lands and that made very good workers. They were capable of handling the simple implements of mowing, and could drive the oxen or the "four-horse team" as well as whites.[135]

In 1861, the Territorial Governor of Nevada recommended to the Commissioner of Indian Affairs that Pah-Ute Indians be supplied with cows, sheep, meat, clothing, ox teams, and farming implements.[136] He thought that with supervision by dedicated employees, and with education for the younger ones, the Pah-Utes could be a successful people within five years, because this was an industrious tribe.

Indian agents discovered that drought years which parched the land caused poor farming conditions on the reservation, and federal aid to supply necessary farming implements was slow to materialize for the willing workers. Agent Jacob L. Lockhart told of the Indians' trek to the mountains to seek native foods, because the Indians were dissatisfied with the improper farming conditions. However, some Indians were asked to remain to plant vegetables.[137] Superintendent T. T. Dwight, contrary to Dodge, said that few Indians of the Pyramid Lake Reservation were willing to work, but that they occupied themselves gathering their native food.[138]

Superintendent Parker recommended that the Indians be taught husbandry so that they could not starve or steal and also urged that the farming appropriations from Congress be more liberal. He commented that the Indians "were willing workers, and easily taught."[139] Agent Campbell said no land was being cultivated, but the Indians were industriously engaged in fencing the arable land while waiting for government aid.[140] H. G. Parker said "The Paiutes have not been able to make as much progress in farming as I could wish."[141] In 1871, there was a report that the Indians of the Pyramid Lake region were starving. The new agent found no one starving, although he could see no sign of the money appropriated for use on the reservation.[142]

Agent Bateman said that in 1875, more acres of land had been put into cultivation than in any previous year, and that "some of the finest ranches in Nevada are upon this reservation, claimed and cultivated by Indians."[143] Agent Barnes reported in 1878 that there was a good yield of crops,[144] so apparently better farming methods were paying off.

Agent Bateman said the Pyramid Lake Reservation land was difficult to irrigate, because it was above the water mark and had sink holes. It was necessary to dig a long ditch to the land. The original ditch that had been built at great expense was useless.

Agent Garvey recommended the building of a large ditch, under the supervision of an engineer, for the Pyramid Lake Reservation. In other years, work on the ditch had been accomplished without survey, and hence was unscientific and inadequate. He believed an adequate ditch, assuring an abundance of water, would induce many Indians to return to the reservation.

At the insistence of the agents, the irrigation system was repaired and rebuilt. In 1881, the Indians built three miles of ditch, helped to build a flume, cut and hauled logs, and put up two abutments and a pier for a two-span bridge across the Truckee River.[145] In 1883, they built a two mile ditch for which they received no cash, only rations for themselves. The team was paid two dollars a day for sixty-six days to haul heavy timber and stores to the river bank for repairs to the dam. In 1894, there was damage to the dam and ditches by early, heavy, and continuous rain and snow.[146] The high waters also spoiled some of the crops however, there was an excellent crop of hay. In 1899, Agent Spriggs related the expenditure of $6,500 on the new dam. When the necessary appropriation for this was received, the old dam was destroyed.[147]

Not until 1910 did Congress pass an act that outlined the necessary preliminary surveys and estimated costs for the Federal irrigation project at the Pyramid Lake Reservation. There would be specialized engineers to supervise the building of the irrigation system. Annual reports of the functioning of this irrigation project would be made to Congress by the Secretary of the Interior.[148]

In the years 1916 through 1918, there were appropriations amounting to $85,000 for improvement, enlargement, and extension of the irrigation system on the Pyramid Lake Reservation.[149] The dam and the irrigation system are in the Nixon area of the reservation.

Agent Garvey said that many Indians had been leaving the reservation because of the crop failures caused by the lack of irrigation, the white man's encroachment upon the fisheries, and the inadequate appropriations.[150] The remaining Indians were horse owners who stayed to protect pasture lands from the white ranchers' cattle. The Kuyui Dokado remained, because they did not wish to leave their birthplace. The transplanted Indians, those who belonged to other Paiute bands but who were forced to live on the reservation, readily left to work in the railroad and mining towns.

In 1881, many Indians wanted to farm, but were discouraged because of the lack of water for irrigation. Some, however, raised onions, tomatoes, beets, cabbage, lettuce, parsnips, cucumbers, melons, radishes, and sweet corn in their gardens. Two hundred tons of hay and eight tons of wheat and barley were reaped from all the farms.[151]

The Federal government employed a farmer to instruct the adult Indians and the school children in 1885. The school had a farm where the children learned the practical arts of farming. The instructor taught them how to raise stock and to farm. He helped to plant fruit trees at the boarding school farm and on the individual Indian farms. There were 1,200 apple trees, 100 cherry trees, 100 peach trees, 100 pear trees, and 100 plum trees. These were from one to four years in growth at the time of planting. The Indians were pleased with their own orchards and took good care of them,[152] but of the 1,600 fruit trees planted, only 600 survived the first winter.[153]

Crop yield was restricted because the reservation had limited agricultural lands, and many good lands were held by old Indians who did not farm. The young Indians, who respected their elders, would not request those lands.[154] But in 1891, the new agent divided the arable lands held by the older Indians among the younger ones to farm. The agent felt he was rewarded in the fall when he saw those fields in grain, hay, and gardens.[155]

During the years 1902 through 1905 there is evidence that at least some Indians were economically enterprising. In 1902, out of an approximate population of 550, there were several individuals who had from ten to twenty head of cattle every year.[156] On his farm, Jim Davis (Indian) had a sign advertising baled hay for sale, while another Indian operated a milk route for regular customers, another operated a blacksmith shop, and another sold beef to both whites and Indians.[157]

On April 13, 1937, the Commissioner of Indian Affairs reported to the Senate Indian Affairs Committee that on the Pyramid Lake Indian Reservation, the largest land unit tilled by one family was twenty-six acres, while the smallest unit of tilled land was two and one-half acres. He said each Indian family there should have twenty to twenty-six acres of land and from

Two women carrying wood from the Truckee River Land, 1870-80, Wadsworth, Nevada.
Courtesy of Harry Huston

twenty to forty head of cattle.[158] At that time, fifty-two Indians owned 1,050 beef cattle, sixteen Indians owned twenty-five dairy cattle, and fifty-six owned 214 horses. The average calf crop in 1935 was sixty-five percent. Six Indians owned a total of 149 turkeys, and thirty-one owned 946 other poultry.

The chairman of the Pyramid Lake Tribal Council disclosed that only 636 acres of farming land was irrigable in 1943.[159] Seventy families operated these acres, so that the average farm contained nine acres. He estimated the cattle on the reservation to be 1,500. Most of the heads of families had ten cattle with which to start a herd.[160] Albert Mauwee, Tribal Secretary, said he owned forty-five to fifty head of cattle, and there was range for them, but they had to be fed in the winter.[161]

In 1959, the Fulcher report reiterated that the Indians had the oldest water rights on the Truckee River, (See Chapter III on Legislation). But since other farmers and town groups were taking water from the river, the Indians were not receiving their share. In 1944, 3,133 acres of bench land on Dodge Flat between Wadsworth and Nixon was granted in the final decree.[162] No diversion canal was constructed to carry water to Dodge Flat, as it would have been a very expensive project. At the time of the study, the irrigated lands on the reservation totaled 600 acres, although 1,200 acres had been irrigated. Erosion cut the irrigated acreage to its present area. The Indians farmed the tribal assigned fields of three to thirty acres. Winter food for cattle was raised on these tracts, and there were produce gardens. Livestock was the most extensive agricultural activity.[163]

In the years since 1947 agriculture has been on the decline on the reservation. Only the land lately received from the white claimants in Wadsworth was of economic value as the other farms were small. Reasons for the agricultural decline were the increased cost of farming, inadequate implements, lack of credit, land erosion, and job opportunities off the reservation.[164]

The Central Pacific Railroad

In 1868 when the Central Pacific Railroad extended into the southern part of the Pyramid Lake Indian Reservation, it created problems. The Indians were unhappy when they learned that the railroad was to be on the reservation for previous experiences had demonstrated that Indians residing in proximity to the whites were adversely affected.[165] Recognizing this problem, J. P. Usher, representative of the Department of the Interior, recommended that six miles be deducted from the southern portion of the reservation so that the Indians would not be near the railroad and the town of white people.[166]

In spite of the Indians' reluctance to join the whites in the railroad town of Wadsworth, then the principal town of the district, conditions of the reservation impelled many of them to move near the railroad. Farm crops on the reservation failed, and hundreds of Indians left for the town to earn subsistence for their families.[167] By 1890, one-fourth of the reservation population was on the outskirts of the town of Wadsworth. Since no farm acreage was available to them, the Indian men worked as yard workers, wood choppers, house men doing the heavy house cleaning and railroad and farm labors, while the women were house servants who did the laundry either in the whites' homes or at their own homes. At the time, half of the reservation's tillable land in the Wadsworth area was occupied by white "squatters,"[168] still further undermining the ability of the Indians to earn a living by farming.

Meanwhile the Indians and whites in Wadsworth achieved a certain rapport. Their attitude towards one another was one of appreciation, friendship, and mutual reliance. The Indians depend largely for their survival on the remuneration for their labor from white employers. White and Indian workers, being side by side taught each other their languages. Many whites in the Wadsworth area spoke Paiute as fluently as any Paiute, while most Paiute understood and spoke English.[169]

The Indians of the Pyramid Lake Reservation were reported to be cooperative with the road, so were given free rides on the Central Pacific.[170] The reservation agents were unfavorable to the arrangement, as the Indians readily dropped their working implements to attend a pow-wow in Winnemucca or a Fourth of July celebration in San Francisco by way of the railroad.[171] They also

Central Pacific Railroad Depot and Business District of Wadsworth, Nevada – 1901.
Postcard addressed to Mr. Frank Ackley, Wadsworth, Nevada, and post-
marked Olinghouse, Nevada, Dec. 4, 1905 (1¢ postage).
Courtesy of Marjorie Ackley MacArthur

went to the Sacramento area to pick hops in season, but would not return to put their children into the scheduled reservation schools.[172] They were reported to be thriftless and drunk in the California towns; consequently the agents requested the railroad stop the free rides.[173] The agents' requests went unheeded by the railroad for many years, but in the second decade of this century, free rides were discontinued because of a wreck in which some Indian riders were killed and others injured.[174] When the railroad moved its site of operation from Wadworth to Sparks, many reservation Indians followed it to that city.[175]

Although the Indians did not realize the importance of the passage of the railway through their reservation when it was originally built, the railroad eventually came to play a most important role in their lives. Unaware of its potentialities, they failed to understand that the United States would be linked from the East coast to the West for the first time when the Central Pacific Railroad met the Union Pacific Railroad at Promontory, Utah, near Ogden in May 1869.

The entrance of the railroad on the reservation gave the Indians the impetus to work as individuals, undermining the traditional dependence upon a paternal United States government. Realizing the inadequacy of the governmental farming program to them, many went to make their living outside the reservation.

The United States government sponsored a Relocation Program in 1952 for the young Indian to move to the large urban areas of California and Nevada for work. This necessitated their adjusting to city life as living conditions in the low rent housing areas were crowded and unlike the spacious Reservation land.

The Neh-muh began to work on a reform of the Bureau of Indian Affairs programs for the reservation. If good housing could be established, they could still live on the land cherished by their older people and commute to wherever work was available nearby. This was a plan more agreeable to the elders, who always resented the transfer of their children to distant lands for schooling and lately to strange cities for work.

Greater reform, with government aid, is necessary to rectify the diminishing waters of the Truckee River and to assist the young people in developing the Tubewah as a productive and liveable homesite for both young and old.

CHAPTER IX

Education and Social Change (1859-1959)

On Frémont's second trip through Nevada, Truckee, who was then a band leader, and a number of other Paiutes accompanied him to California. One of the great impressions received by the Indians there was the importance of the schools for the white children. Before Truckee's death, he obtained a promise that his granddaughters, Sarah Winnemucca and her sister, would be taken to a friend in California, where the girls would be schooled.[176]

Subsequently the Paiutes requested schools for their children, and generally the local officials honored their requests. Governor of the Nevada Territory and Superintendent of Indian Affairs, James W. Nye, said schools were a necessity for the Indians, and the Paiutes of Nevada should be taught "reading, writing ... farming, spinning and weaving, preserving meats and grains."[177] Warren Wasson, Acting agent, wrote that "... of all the Indians I am acquainted with, the most susceptible of acquiring the arts of civilized life are the Paiutes,"[178] although Agent Batemen reported on September 30, 1871, that he thought food was far more important than the school the Paiutes were demanding for their children.[179]

Plans for educating the Indians were gradually developed. In 1878, the Secretary of the Interior reported that vocational schools were being established on the Indian reservations, and that the English language would be used to impart elementary and practical knowledge.[180]

When school opened on the Pyramid Lake Reservation, March 1, 1878, eighteen students were in attendance. The other children, who helped their parents and relatives obtain food, were not in school, and Agent Barnes recommended that students be given subsistence so they could attend school. He regarded the improvement of the Pah-Ute children in "intelligence and morality" as his most important work.[181]

When the day school started the next year, fifty-two children were enrolled.[182] The school met in a large room of the Agency building.[183] That year, the attendance was irregular, but those in regular attendance showed much progress. It was noted that there was no difference in capacity for learning between Caucasian and Indian children. Because of the irregular attendance of the students, Agent W.M. Garvey in 1880 recommended a boarding school; but funds were not made available until 1882.[184]

When the children started the school farm in 1883, the parents helped by taking their teams to haul supplies and lumber. They cleared the brush on the selected farm lands; then they leveled and fenced it.[185] When the day school was started, the school farm was an extracurricular activity for the children. Later it fitted properly into the boarding school curriculum.

The boarding school was built on high ground on approximately the same site as the Public School area of 1959, Nixon, Nevada. It opened in September, 1885 with emphasis on vocational education. A teacher, a matron, an assistant matron, and an industrial teacher were employed. The children attended regularly and learned the traditional subjects (reading, writing, and spelling) but they preferred to draw and sing.[186] The boys liked musical instruments, and after school practiced on the organ. Outside the regular school work, they kept busy on the school farm. The school boys raised 1,500 pounds of potatoes, 300 pumpkins, 200 squash, 2,000 pounds of turnips, 2,000 pounds of beets and carrots, 3,000 melons, 200 head of cabbage, and 1,000 pounds of onions.[187] The girls made aprons, pillow cases, dresses, sheets, shawls, shirts, towels, undergarments, and boys' shirts. They mended, cooked, and cleaned house. The boys were apprenticed to the carpenter, and they learned fast. Courses in hygiene, geography, and arithmetic we added to the curriculum of the Pyramid Lake Boarding School in 1888.[188]

The children were very obedient, and within two years there were no occasions for whipping or slapping. Agent W. D. C. Gibson said, "Unlike white children, it is seldom that they quarrel among themselves; never fight, and from school age up, it is a rare thing hear one cry."[189]

In 1887, the school was filled to capacity. Ten boys who had completed the curriculum at the Pyramid Lake Boarding School went to Grand Junction, Colorado, to further their education. The agent regretted that the boys had left, because the parents mourned them as though they were dead.[190] This anguish of Indians who separated from their children was a strong argument in favor of an advanced school in the state.

In 1886 Agent Gibson of Pyramid Lake informed the state officials of this need for an advanced school. As a result, the Thirteenth Legislature of Nevada

Day School Children, Wadsworth, Nevada (1910). Building was resident of
Indian Deputy Police (1899); St. Michaels and All Saints Church (1959).

passed an Act in 1887 to establish an Indian school with the proceeds of a
$10,000 bond issue. Pressure for schools came, also, from the Indians and white
citizens of the Washoe and Shoshone areas of the state. An "Indian School
Commission" was created to purchase land and to establish the school.[191]

The land purchased was three miles south of Carson City, and it comprised 240 acres. The school was called the Clear Creek Indian School. Later
it was known as Carson Indian School. It was an industrial school where the
girls learned home economic subjects and the boys trade subjects. In 1890,
the Federal government bought the new school property from the state. As
United States Senator William Stewart from Nevada was instrumental in the
purchase, the school was named the Stewart Indian School in his honor, and
was located with a post office at Stewart, Nevada.[192] This school, besides stim-
ulating intellectual growth, also dispelled prejudices of the three tribes whose
children were in attendance.

Another school was necessary on the Pyramid Lake Reservation. One-fourth
of the reservation Indians lived on the outskirts of Wadsworth, the railroad town
on the reservation. They could have moved to the agency to put their children in
school, but no land was available to them. So another school was created on the
reservation at Wadsworth when the parents objected to separation from their
children.[193] The day school started in April 1891, and was held in the agency
building near the Indian village. One teacher taught the beginning classes.[194]

Later, a dining room was added to the school building so the children could be fed the noon meal.[195] The teacher at the Pyramid Lake Agency regretted the addition of the dining room, as he though the children should be in residence at the Agency boarding school, and thus be isolated from the unfavorable atmosphere of the village. The Wadsworth Indian School was closed on May 17, 1893.[196] One of the reasons for its closing was that the children would run to the train depot to see the trains come in. They received pittances in food and money from the passengers. In the fall of 1899, it was reopened,[197] but in 1921 it was permanently closed, because with the transfer of the Central Pacific Railroad to Sparks, Wadsworth rapidly declined and many Indian families, moved.[198]

From the turn of the century, some Indian students successfully attended public schools in the towns of Carson and Reno, so when the Federal government asked the local school boards to integrate Indian students into public schools there was not much dissension. Indian children were capable of doing the regular school work of the Nevada curriculum for the elementary and high schools. Because they had the same abilities and learning variations as non-Indian children, the Indian children were integrated into the Nevada Public Schools. In 1948, the Nevada Day School at Pyramid Lake Agency was accepted into the Nevada Public School System. The school was named Nahtze, the Paiute word for "boy" and the name of one son of Chief Winnemucca. At the same time, new educational concepts regarding Indian children were made. The assimilation of the Indian children into the Public Schools of Nevada can be rated as the highest in the West.[199]

From the Pyramid Lake Reservation, the high school students attended the Fernley High School; the upper elementary graded students, the Wadsworth school; and the primary graded students, Nixon. Federal post-high schools and state colleges and universities are available to students who desire further education. All the children now attend the Public Schools of Nevada with the exception of orphans or delinquents who may attend the Federal school at Stewart.

Law and Order

The Paiute band life was orderly, so the Kuyui Dokado did not request the white man's form of law and order. The Kuyui Dokado behaved well after the difficulties of the Pyramid Lake Wars of 1860. When white men shot at some Indians and then took their ponies, and when other outrages were done to them, the Indians did not retaliate. Many of the conflicts reported during the early 1860's between the Indians and the whites were exaggerated. Hoping to keep the Indians peaceable in the face of white depredation, General Wright sent them flour and meat from San Francisco.[200]

Pyramid Lake Indian Reservation Police – 1883.
Left to Right: Captain Dave, Jack Samuels, John Smith, Joe Mandel, Willie Biscuit sta-
tioned at Nixon, Nevada. Jigger Bob, Rawhide Henry (not in picture) stationed West
Pyramid Lake. James Shaw (not in picture) stationed Wadsworth, Nevada.

There was sobriety on the reservation; intoxicated Indians were those who loitered in the railroad and mining towns.[201] Agent Spencer said,

> I was happily disappointed in finding the Pah-Ute Indians no band of wild, stolid, game hunting semisavages, but a tribe of peaceable, intelligent, agricultural people as much inclined to labor as most white men would be under similar circumstances.[202]

Yet for some, submission to the white men's code was very difficult. Some did not realize that when a person planted and raised a crop, the yield belonged to the farmer.[203] They believed that whatever grew underground was common property as the potatoes in the mountains. The agent felt the taking of farm produce resulted from ignorance rather than criminal intent; however, he thought the Indians taking another's crop should be arrested and detained for a day or two so that they would realize that such action was considered stealing. Agent Spencer put in a request for police and a guard house, since the reservation lacked both, stating further that the guard house and police would be warranted by the drunkenness which occasionally would occur. He said the Indian police could evict trespassers on the reservation. The guard house was shortlived as by 1892 there was a report from the agent that it was not needed.[204]

James Shaw, Indian Deputy Police – 1899
Wadsworth, Nevada.

In 1883, the newly created police force included one captain and six privates.[205] The captain was Numana Dave, and the privates were Jack Samuels, John Smith, Joe Mandel, Willie Biscuit, Rawhide Henry, and Jigger Bob. Jigger Bob served on the west side of Pyramid Lake. In 1888, Agent Gibson described them as "prompt, reliable, efficient, and sober men."[206] The salary of each was $10-$15 per month. In 1891, James Shaw was detailed as a deputy to Wadsworth to help the town official, an arrangement which proved beneficial.[207]

Federal officials created a federal court to try offenders who committed crimes on the reservation. Agent Sears said of the Pyramid Lake Court Members,

> . . . three intelligent, middle-aged Pah-Utes, whose wise and impartial decisions would, in many instances, put to shame those rendered by courts of much higher repute.[208]

The agent thought the Indian court was one of the most important means in securing civilization. Since the judges were impartial and unselfish, the Indians respected their opinion and authority, and obeyed their judgment.

A record taken over approximately twenty years shows the following statistics: In 1883, there were four arrests, three for trivial offenses, one for assault. The trivial offenses drew reprimands; the assault resulted in three days in the guard house. In 1886, fourteen were arrested; of the three arrested for intoxication one was acquitted while two received 30-day jail terms; three assaults resulted in one acquittal, one three day jail plus two weeks' work in the fields; one assault and battery case spent thirty days in jail; in two property damage suits, one was convicted and the other acquitted; one divorce by mutual consent, and three rights to property of deceased were adjusted. In 1888, there were three arrests: one for wife beating, one horse killing, and one murder. The murderer was jailed in Carson. From 1889 through 1898 there were no serious crimes. With the decline of Wadsworth there was no deputy in 1905.[209]

By the Congressional Act of June 28, 1932, Indians who committed any of the major crimes of murder, manslaughter, incest, arson, burglary, robbery, larceny, assault with a dangerous weapon, or assault with intent to kill were made subject to the same court laws, and manners, with the same penalties as other persons within the United States jurisdiction, while rape was punishable according to the court of the state wherein it was committed.[210]

Health
Early reports, around 1861, concerning the health of the Pyramid Lake Indians, were good. Of course, there were minor illnesses, infirmities due to old age, and

Eugene Frazier's Canee made of Straw, Nixon, Nevada, 1910.
Eugene Frazier, Mr. Creel, Mattie Natches, (?).
Courtesy of Nina and Willie Smith

accidents. Warren Wasson, the acting agent at that time, requested a medicine chest from the Commissioner of Indian Affairs.[211] Superintendent Parker reported that, because the Paiutes were better fed than the surrounding tribes, they were "better developed, both physically and mentally."[212] He said there were a few deaths from smallpox and some from fever near the sinks of the rivers. Otherwise the health of the Nevada Indians was good.[213] In 1872, the health of the Indians was reported to have improved since earlier reports, because of better housing, better preparation of food, and increased provision for clothing. There were some cases of inflammation of the eyes. The agent believed the sore eyes were caused by the "tatooing" of the faces with mineral paints.

It was not until 1874 that the Bureau of Indian Affairs requested well-trained physicians for the Indian reservations.[214] Twelve years expired before the request was granted; in 1886 a resident physician was appointed for medical aid. That year the Pah-Utes made 300 calls on his services.[215] In one year, Dr. R. Webber served several hundred Indians whose health was generally good. In that year, there were 44 births of 22 males and 22 females and there were no deaths.[216]

About 1880 some of the Indians, whose traditional faith in the medicine men was shaken, began to go for medicine from the medical stores of the agency;[217] but many Indians still hired the medicine men. Horses were killed to make feasts for the relatives who assisted the medicine men in the performance

Transition House, 1870-1880. Wadsworth, Nevada.
Courtesy of Harry Huston

of the ritual for the sick. For remuneration the shamans were given treasured items. Because of this, it was thought that the singing of the medicine men over the sick as part of the Pah-Ute religion was for selfish and mercenary reasons.[218] In 1889, Agent S.S. Sears reported the medicine men still ruled as "prophet, priest, and king."[219] However, by 1959 there were no practicing shamans on the reservation.

On March 4, 1915, Congress approved plans for a new hospital to be built in Carson. Ninety thousand dollars was appropriated for the building and ten thousand dollars for its maintenance. The Indians of Pyramid Lake who needed hospitalization could utilize this hospital.[220] During World War II, when the hospital could not be staffed, the equipment was transferred to the Walker River Hospital, and the Pyramid Lake patients were cared for there.

In 1925, a tuberculosis sanitarium was built and operated on the reservation by the Federal government.[221] The site was chosen because of climatic conditions, not because of the high rate of the disease on the Pyramid Lake Reservation. The building appropriations came in three installments:[222] the first, $30,000; the second, $25,000; and the third, including an x-ray machine, $28,000.[223] This sanitarium was available to tubercular patients from the Western States. Ten years later, this sanitarium was abandoned.[224]

The health of the Pyramid Lake Indians about 1912 was referred to by a former Federal employee, Mrs. Janette Woodruff, who said,

Tuberculosis was the scourge of the Papagos as it was of the Crows. The Paiutes seemed to be freer of diseases of all kinds than either of the other tribes, though I cannot assign reason for the fact.[225]

The Public Health Service under the administration of the Surgeon General of the United States started operation of all Indian Service hospitals on July 1, 1954. The Walker River Hospital at Schurz began to operate under the new setup.[226]

Up to 1959 on the reservation, a few families occupied good modern homes with running water, plumbing, and electricity for modern appliances, but most of them occupied houses of two-rooms which were crowded and in need of repair. About five persons lived in one unit. Most of the water supply was from wells and springs which were unprotected. Sewage disposal was inadequate.[227]

The Ghost Dance

The Shaman could have more than one power. Supposedly, a vision gave him his songs. For his paraphanelia he had sticks, feathers, eagle's down, dew claw rattle, rawhide rattle, and paints. He prayed to his personal spirit, to the sun, and to the ghost which was visible to him. The ghost traveled in the whirlwind and was feared. Ordinary people dreaming of ghosts could nullify dreams by a cold bath, a smoke, or a prayer.

At the circle dances a shaman would tell of his visions. After the dances there were bathing ceremonies. The dancers painted themselves with the earth paints.

When the Ghost Dance, was originated by Wodziwob (Grey Hair) about 1869, the procedure was not new. Wodziwob came from Mason Valley as did the other two famous Ghost Dance shamans. Gilbert Natchez, of the Kuyui Dokado said Wodziwob was the same age as Sarah Winnemucca so he must have been born approximately in 1844. Wodziwob went to the Kuyui country advocating the return of all the dead at the Ghost Dance. When the dead did not return the Kuyui Dokado lost faith in this shaman. Wodziwob left.

Another prophet, Weneygua (standing-up) with the English name of Frank Spencer, came and lived with the Pyramid group for five years. He made several trips to Oregon to visit the Paiutes living with the Modoc. He was the shaman who acquainted those Indians with the Ghost Dance.

Pete Polina told Cora Du Bois that there never were threats to the cynics and the whites. He thought the people fainted from weakness after five nights of dancing rather than being in a trance.

The Kuyui group was one of the bands which denounced the Ghost Dance theory. It believed the shamans were curers rather than prophets. It did not believe in Jack Wilson's prophecy. Its belief was that rain making was shamanistic and not prophetic.

Cora Du Bois said,[228] "In strict accuracy I feel that it is misleading to speak of the Paviotos Ghost Dances with the Connotation attached to them to the Californian and Plains (1890) manifestations. The behavior patterns which became attached to these cults outside of Western Nevada were not necessary correlates of an adventist doctrine among the Paviotso. Foreign tribes in accepting the prophecies not only placed them in a new concept, but also attached to them Paviotos traits which were merely in solution among the originators."

Religious Acculturation

Christian missionary work among the Paiutes was neglected in Nevada prior to 1875. In 1872, Agent Batemen requested religious missionaries, saying the Paiutes "were superstitiously benighted so far as true religion is concerned but not blind to their sense of honor."[229]

Under the denominational allotment plan by which the Federal government assigned religious denomination preference to name an agent and to work on assigned Indian reservations, the Baptists nominated an Indian Agent at the Pyramid Lake Reservation in 1875.[230] Reverend J. M. Helsey, Baptist missionary served on the reservation although he lived in Wadsworth and traveled to Nixon to hold services. The adult Indians were very attentive and they liked him.[231]

The Episcopal Church for the Kuyui Dokado was started with the Right Reverend Bishop Leonard of Reno, the Reverend T. L. Bellam, the missionary pastor at Wadsworth, and Miss Marion Taylor the resident missionary.[232] This group formed the first Indian Church in Nevada.[233] Services were first held in a government building. The year following the first service, eight adults and thirty-two children were baptized.

The original Episcopal Church for the Paiutes was built in 1896; in 1912 it was destroyed in a fire. The next Episcopal Church at Nixon was forty-four feet by seventy-two feet, with a seating capacity of 200 people. The vicarage, a frame building, was built in 1917 as a memorial to Bishop Spaulding. Joseph Hall, the parish hall, was erected in 1932. These buildings were the physical properties of the Episcopal Mission at Nixon. At Wadsworth, the government school building was used for services until 1934. After renovation the name given was "Saint Michaels and All Angels Church." There were two Episcopal Churches on the reservation. Since the Paiute Indians accepted the Christian Faith without totally abandoning their true religion, they were thought to have two faiths, "He held them as separate entities to be kept apart and used, each when it was needed."[234] The Indians were believed to esteem the white man's doctor, and the Indian's medicine man.

Gambling in Wadsworth town 1870-1880.
Picture courtesy of Harry Huston with notation "man in white shirt is your father, James Shaw."

An Episcopalian minister who served on the Pyramid Lake Reservation, Father Joseph Hogben, was called the "Buckaroo Priest," because he visited his parishioners on a horse. He came in 1937, and left to be a chaplain in World War II. He later returned to the reservation in 1956.[235]

For five years in the absence of Father Hogben, Gareth Hughes, the ex-Shakespearean Hollywood actor, came to the Pyramid Lake Reservation as a lay worker, known as Brother David. He was given much publicity in the new role. Many Indians appreciated his mission work, but most doubted his sincerity.[231]

In 1958, the Episcopal Church membership on the reservation was ninety-nine. In that year, the baptisms numbered fourteen. Sunday school and Sunday morning service attendance totaled fifty each. One hundred seventy-three attended other types of weekly services. The total weekly attendance of all groups was 275.[237]

On the reservation, the Episcopalian Church has made the greatest effort to reach the Indians, and its acceptance of Indians in an integrated church has been greater than that of some other Protestant bodies. Probably the Indian, used to the shaman's ceremonies, enjoyed the ritualistic ceremony of the Episcopal Church for, while its ritual is not as dramatic as that of the Roman

Father Hogben and Boy Scouts of America Troop. He was an active leader in this program.
Courtesy of Mrs. Joseph Hogben

Reverend Joseph Hogben, known as the "Buckaroo Priest," feeding the horse he rode to visit parishioners. Courtesy of Mrs. Joseph Hogben.

Catholic Church, it was more readily understood by the Indians because it was conducted in the English language. In the opinion of the Reverend George W. Smart, however, the missionary work in Nevada was slow[238] and even the Episcopalians "had lean years for the first decade or more."

Twenty years had elapsed since the Indians' first contact with the white men before they learned of Christianity. Too many harsh experiences with the whites aroused skepticism towards Biblical words of brotherly love. Indian children were admonished by their parents to accept only the mode of the white civilization that would be beneficial and to cling to the fine characteristics of the Paiute credo.

Peyote

The Peyote cult had been in use by the Northern Indian tribe of the United States for at least 200 years. Originally it was a native ceremony used in Mexico and the southern United States by the American Indians. In this ceremony the peyote (cactus bud) was used.

The peyote (Lophophora williamsii) is a species of cacti which possesses narcotic properties. The top is about five inches in diameter. The mescal buttons form on the top of the plant, which are cut, dried, and used by the cult members.

The intoxication caused by this drug has two phases: first, the period of contentment and deep sensitivity; second, the period of nervousness combined with sluggish muscles, causing "hypocerebrality, colored hallucination and synaesthesia."[239]

It (peyote) was eaten, chewed or drunk during prayers; sage leaves then were massaged on the body while cedar smoke was fanned over the body-ritual equipment. The body was touched, and special water was put on; then cigarettes were smoked.[240]

The Pyramid Lake Indians experimented with the use of peyote in 1929-30 when Leo Okio, an Eastern Indian, met with them. The Indians were impressed when Okio seemingly cured a case of pneumonia and paralysis; however, the Indians were more impressed with the fact that Okio took much money with him when he left.[241]

In 1936, Ben Lancaster, from the Washoe tribe, had peyote meetings on the Pyramid Lake Reservation. Many sickly Indians tried the peyote for cure. Most of them were not cured, but died from their illness.

Thirteen people were named as participants in the newly introduced cult in 1929 at Pyramid Lake. Four named in the list were Coleville, California, residents; one was the leader of the cult for the area. In 1959, there were members of one household who still used peyote. The California leader came to hold meetings with this family on the reservation.[242]

Thus the peyote cult, introduced to the Pyramid Lake Indians in 1929-30 by Leo Okio, an Eastern Indian, did not thrive. There were only about four members in 1959. The Indians were seeking a cure for ailments and when not satisfactorily cured, abandoned the cult.

World War I

During World War I, most of the American Indians were not subject to the draft. They were not at that time considered citizens of the United States. Volunteers were accepted if they passed the tests required.[243] The following six men from the Pyramid Lake Reservation served in· this war: Cubit Rhoades, Cheyenne Aleck, William W. Shaw, Hastings Pancho, Jim Dewey, and William Bridges.

The older Indians knew there was a war across a large body of water, and they consented to let the young men volunteer their services in spite of their own fears of war. While the men were gone, the Indians became more aware of the news of the day. They congregated at the post office to hear talk about news from papers. The men admonished their women when they wept aloud, a traditional expression of sorrow. The mothers and relatives of the soldiers were told to concentrate on hope and faith that the young men would return safely to the reservation.

When the boys returned from "over there," some sought to finish their education at Stewart, while others started their life work in the communities on and off the reservation. Some joined the American Legion and the Veterans of Foreign Wars, and were active participants during their lifetime. They were active in Memorial Day and other national holidays, and at veterans' funerals. They erected a flag pole at the two Wadsworth cemeteries, where the flag could be displayed on memorial occasions. The veterans were inspirational to later war veterans. Hastings Pancho helped to organize an Indian Veterans' Band at Nixon. This band participated in many reservation activities, and at celebrations in Reno, Fallon, Sparks, and Carson City. It was still active in 1959, although the original members were gone. Later recruits were from other places such as Reno, Sparks, Carson City, and Fallon. This group of men with other Indian veterans of World War I were instrumental in acquiring citizenship for all American Indians in the United States by the Act of June 2, 1924 (Chapter III).

World War II

Because of the special 1924 enactment that granted them citizenship, American-born Indians were subject to the Selective Service in World War II.

By 1941, there were many American Indians in the National Guard units, and some of these were among the first moved to the battlefields. The Indians made outstanding soldiers, and because of their quick movements and tradition of scouting, they readily fit into the new military tactics of rapid mobility.

At the beginning of this war, because the Indians had been discriminated against, there was a question as to how they would respond to the clash of ideologies. In three states they could not vote; in industrial employment they were the last to get a job and the first to go; and they were barred from civic action, because they lacked funds to hire the best lawyers to defend them. Because of their minority status, the Indians did not receive fair trials. However, they

PFC. Francis Shaw, son of Hattie and Dennis Shaw, born February 19,
1915, killed in action August 5, 1943, World War II – Sicily.

responded enthusiastically to the call to take up arms for their country; adults and children bought United States War bonds and stamps, and many left the reservations to work in the war industries.[244]

The Pyramid Lake Indians responded as did other Indians of the United States before and during the World War II. In 1943, when the Pyramid Lake Council delegates appealed to the Congressional hearings for the reservation lands that were proposed to be given to white settlers (in Bill S. 24), the Council Secretary reported there were forty boys in the armed services who would want land when they returned.[245] The Chairman of the Council, in his testimony for those lands cited, "you find the blood of the American Indians—the Pyramid Lake Indians—on every battle front."[246]

Two half-brothers who died in the African war area were from the Pyramid Lake Reservation.[247] Francis Shaw, infantryman, received the Silver Star medal, posthumously. He was mortally wounded in Sicily while scouting ahead of his unit.[248] Arthur Jones died when his airplane was shot down over Corsica.

Arthur Shaw Jackson, native of Nixon, Nevada, returned home after the war. He received thirty-two decorations from five countries in the European theatre of war. Included in his decorations were:

> . . . the Distinguished Service Cross, the Silver Star, the Purple Heart with five Oak Leaf Clusters, the Bronze Star with One Oak Leaf Cluster, the Soldier's Medal, the Combat Infantry Badge, and the Distinguished Unit Badge with four Clusters, all from the United States. He also won the Croix de Guerre of France, Belgium, Holland, and Luxemberg. He was called "Nevada's Most Decorated Service Man."[249]

In the Korean War there were sixteen stars on the Pyramid Lake Reservation service flag in 1952. Several men did not return.[250]

After the Korean War, the women expanded their activities by organizing an A.W.V.S. unit. The All-American Unit of the American Women's Voluntary Service was installed at the Pyramid Lake Reservation on October 27, 1957. It was the first Indian group in the National organization. The group participated in activities at the Reno hospitals, the U.S.O., and the Pyramid Lake Reservation.[251]

The next year, the Chairman of the group carried a letter from Governor Charles H. Russell to the National A.W.V.S. convention in Chicago. The letter was an invitation to the members of the organization to attend the 1959 convention, which was to be held in Reno.[252]

For the men, one of the main effects of World War II and the Korean War was that the veterans with their friends felt the Indians were discriminated against when they could not go into public houses to purchase any alcoholic drinks. So by the Act of August 15, 1953, the Indian Liquor Law was passed to eliminate discriminatory legislation against Indians who wished to purchase alcoholic drinks.[253]

By these and other methods the Kuyui Dokado band has progressed economically, educationally, and politically toward full citizenship.

Street Scene, Wadsworth, Nevada, 1902.

CHAPTER X

The Leaders

The Pyramid Lake leaders exemplified the Paiute way of life. They were kind, considerate, generous, and fair minded. Their peacefulness seemed almost a fault.

Truckee

Truckee was a chief of a Northern Paiute band that lived part of the time in the Humboldt and Pyramid Lake areas.[254] He was happy when he heard the white men were approaching. He recollected for his people the legend of the Two Dark and the Two White Children. As the whites advanced from the West, Truckee went to greet them in an effort to show friendliness of the Indians, only to be treated as an unwelcome guest. Although he was disappointed, he said, "Perhaps they'll come next year." Truckee's experience probably was with the Chile's Eastern expedition from California in 1842.[255]

In 1844, Truckee met the Stevens party near the Humboldt Sink. He told the pioneers of a river that was fifty or sixty miles due West, where there were cottonwood trees and good grass.[256] The members of this party gave the name of "Truckee" to the river in gratitude to the friendly guide.

In 1845, Captain Johnson gave Truckee a tin circular piece of which Truckee was so proud he bored holes in it and wore it on his head as a hat. The "hat" was a source of amusement for the soldiers, who laughed when they saw this tin plate on Truckee's head as he joined Frémont on the trip to California.[257] This did not offend him, as he felt it was not meant as ridicule.

During the third summer of the coming of the white man, Captain Frémont and Truckee met at the present site of Wadsworth. It was here that Truckee was given the title of Captain. Truckee and twelve other Indians escorted Frémont over the Sierra when Frémont made his second trip into Nevada.

Truckee and the other Indians stayed in California, and when they returned home they told about the beautiful land. They were proud of their ability to shoot the guns they brought back, of their army uniforms, and especially proud of their ability to speak English. In the fall he returned to California with thirty families. He asked his son, Winnemucca, to be chief in his place. From that time on until his death, his son kept the title. During the winter while Truckee was in California, some emigrants could not pass over the mountains, so they stayed near the Carson River. The Indians carried food to the emigrants without any thought of remuneration, as they believed in sharing with those less fortunate.

Winnemucca, some of the mothers, and older children met Truckee when he returned the second time, because Truckee had specifically asked that no small children be brought since he and his people were bringing guns. He feared the young children would be frightened or killed. He also brought a "paper-rag friend" letter which later introduced him to many whites who befriended him.[258] Later when he knew he was near death, he asked that his "paper-rag friend" be buried with him.

That winter Truckee told of his experiences in California, and he sang the soldiers' bugle calls and the Star Spangled Banner for the people, who in turn learned these songs.

On his third trip to California he took, along with his family, Winnemucca's wife and children. While on this trip, the Indians saw white men whipping Negro wagon-team drivers. Truckee refused to go with this wagon train over the mountains. When his granddaughter became ill after eating too much cake, Truckee admonished his daughter-in-law for not saying a prayer before presenting strange food to her daughter. He explained to his people that when the whites hung their garments on the clothesline, it was to dry them and the clothes were not being cast out; therefore, the Paiutes were not to touch them.

Upon his return to Nevada, Truckee learned of the death of many of his people. All the Indians were mourning aloud. They blamed the deaths upon the water that had been poisoned by the whites. He scolded them, saying his white brothers would not do that. He continued, ". . . don't let your hearts work against your white fathers; if you do, you will not get along."[259]

One day when Truckee, his sons, and his cousins were fishing on the Humboldt River, some whites shot and killed one of his sons. The Indians took the body back to their village, where everyone wept. Truckee explained to the Indians, though weeping, that his word was stronger than his son's death. He had promised never to harm white people.

In 1859 Truckee died. Before his death, his good friend, M. Snyder, promised to take Truckee's two granddaughters to his white friend in California, where those friends would send the girls to school.

Truckee extolled the goodness of the whites, and upheld his promise to the whites even when his son and people suffered at their hands. Thus the Paiute credo of peace with the white brothers worked.

Winnemucca

Winnemucca preferred to continue to live as the Paiutes had lived before the whites came. He had seen the whites do some diabolical acts, and though he realized the whites were here to stay, he did not want his people to have any contacts with them, because the Paiutes had suffered too much at their hands.

When his father, Truckee, left him in charge of the band, Winnemucca took his people to get food for the winter. This was because it was rumored that the whites were ruthlessly killing the Indians,[260] and winter food storage of the Indians was burned by an emigrant party which later, was reported to have been snowed in at the mountain top. Winnemucca told his people to have five days of celebration, then he wanted to relate his dreams to them. After the celebration, he told them he saw many whites on the Humboldt River trail. He said though his father liked them, the whites did not seem to like Indians. He said the burning of their winter supply was wrong. He thought the Indians should retreat again to the mountains until his father returned from California.

Winnemucca was an influential man among all the Paiutes, but he was not considered the chief of the tribe as stated by Dodge in 1859.[261] He traveled with his band to and from the Humboldt area, through the Kuyui country to the Honey Lake area.[262]

These bands were closely knit, and considered themselves one big family. He displayed qualities of true leadership when his brother, Wah-he, was killed by Joaquin in the Walker River district. He was en route to that area when Agent Wasson met him, and told him the details of Wah-he's death. After listening carefully, he returned to his own locale.[263]

Governor Nye and Agent Wasson met with the Indian leaders and some representative Indians at Stony Point. There had been some discussions, but Winnemucca had not arrived. So Nye's party waited another day; then it continued on to Pyramid Lake. There they met Winnemucca, who was just arriving from Honey Lake .

After this meeting, Nye reported: "I found him a most intelligent and appreciative man; one who reasons well, and talks like a prudent, reflective leader."[264] The governor carried on a minute and detailed conversation with Winnemucca. He explained the existing government; its nature, its protective and striking powers, and the necessity for all the residents to obey its laws. He continued by explaining the object of the overland stage route, and the necessity of communication by telegraph.

Winnemucca's band was near Camp McDermitt, because it had had difficulty with the whites in the Honey Lake, California area. Because it was considered a roving band, it was sent to the Malheur Reservation in Oregon. This reservation was opened to the Paiutes in 1867.[265] At first the Indians were happy, because they received tents, farm land, and tools. Sam Parrish was kind and understanding.[266] However, when the new agent reversed Parrish's treatment of the Indians, the band returned to McDermitt. The government was determined that the roving Paiute bands be placed on reservations, so in 1878 part of Winnemucca's band was sent to Yakima, Washington. Winnemucca was old, and did not accompany this group. The Paiutes again were unhappy on the new reservation.

In 1880, Chief Winnemucca with his daughter, Sarah, and two other Paiutes went to Washington, D.C. They asked that their Paiute people be removed to their Nevada home, or the Malheur in Oregon, from the Yakima Reservation, but the Secretary of the Interior refused the removal after General Howard testified how another trip to Malheur would be detrimental to the Paiutes.[267]

Like his father, Winnemucca was a man of peace. He said he never killed any human, only game that could be used for food.[268]

Before his death in 1882,[269] he asked Sarah to tell of the wrongs his people had received from the whites. Mrs. Horace Mann, the editor of Sarah's book said that Winnemucca was a "... truly parental chief of his beloved tribe."[270]

Sarah Winnemucca Hopkins

Sarah Winnemucca was born in the Pyramid Lake area about 1844. Her grandfather was Truckee, who guided Captain John Frémont, and her father was Chief Winnemucca.[271] Her Indian name was Thoc-met-ony interpreted as Shell flower.

After the Pyramid Lake Wars, Sarah acted as an interpreter at Fort McDermitt; she interpreted for the army; then again, for her father's band at the newly created reservation at Malheur, Oregon. She was an interpreter until she reported the sufferings of her people to the army. When the agent heard of her disclosures, he released her from her duties. Her people asked her to intercede for them at Washington, DC. On June 12, 1878, as she started for Nevada, she learned that her band had been captured by the warring Bannocks for the refusal to war against the whites. Sarah, with two other Paiutes, stole into Bannocks' camp and succeeded in leading her people out; their escape was discovered by the Bannocks who subsequently started in pursuit. Sarah hurried ahead of the Paiutes to alert the army to come to the rescue of her people; her desperate horseback ride covered a distance of 223 miles in two days, from June 13 to June 15. When her people were sent to the Yakima Reservation, Washington, Sarah was the interpreter. The agent and local Indians made the Paiutes feel unwelcome. It was then she and her family journeyed again to the Nation's capital to get a permit for the Paiutes' release to their own territory.

Sarah went on to lecture to secure money to get to Washington, DC, to demand changes in policy and some action from the government. Despite her efforts, the Indians' living conditions were only slightly improved. She continued to inform the public of the brutality of the agents and to tell them of the unheeding officials that were in the capitol. She described her people as they had been before their contamination by whites, and told of the pleasing customs she felt they should retain.

She was described as:

> . . . a person of medium height, lively, pert, with expressive eyes, speaking with ease, expressing herself perfectly in good English, able to translate quite naturally the most intimate feelings of her soul that revolted against the injustices of the white man.[272]

Although the agents attacked her character, General Howard and other army officials refuted those attacks.[273]

She married Lieutenant Hopkins in 1881, and in the year 1883, with the help of Mrs. Horace Mann, she wrote "Life Among the Piutes."

Sarah conducted an Indian School near Lovelock, Nevada, for three years; and it was there her first husband died of tuberculosis. After his death, Sarah went to visit her sister in Monida, Montana, where she died on October 16, 1891. Throughout her life, this valiant woman sought peace for all the people, white and Indian, in the Neh-muh Tubewa.

Sarah Winnemucca Hopkins unstintingly gave of her time and energy in her efforts to achieve a peaceable and equitable solution for her people's troubles. The courage, sacrifice, and selflessness this dedicated woman possessed lives on in her rare book.

Captain Dave

Captain Dave was a cousin of Sarah Winnemucca, who held him in small esteem, she said he had been responsible for the ousting of Agent Balcom, and she also said that the title he held was insignificant, since the police could not arrest whites or Indians.[274] He was captain of the police force. The Captain helped the agent put an article in the newspapers requesting all Paiutes return to the reservation. When Captain Dave and six private policemen made a trip to San Francisco carrying a letter from Governor Kinkead in which the Captain was described as an intelligent man, and McMasters was a well-liked agent by the Indians. Sarah declared the trip was for the sole purpose of upholding the agent's position.

Mrs. Woodruff said that in a conversation with Joe Wadsworth (Indian) concerning Captain Dave, she learned he was not the betrayer she had been led to believe, but that he was the Indians' father by the title of Numana.[275] She had heard from other sources that he was unreliable.

Captain Dave was given special credit for his outstanding character and the manner in which he always acted when his services were required.[276] The dam that was in operation in 1959, near Nixon, Nevada, was named for Captain Dave, the Numana.

Though Captain Dave's cousin could not find any words to say in his favor, the other Indians endearingly called him Numana. The government officials had high praise for his character and his cooperation with them.

Numaga

Numaga was the leader of the Kuyui Dokado band in 1860, with no authority elsewhere. The whites called him the "War Chief," although the Paiutes had no chiefs by that title;[277] and they also called him Young Winnemucca, the chief; by this reasoning they considered him a reliable friend.[278] He was cousin to Sarah Winnemucca.[279] His prime concern was to better the living conditions of his people.[280]

When there was talk about war, Numaga traveled from camp to camp to discourage contemplation of it. The Indians answered not; their silence indicated his talks fell on closed ears.

When Numaga was alone, the Old Chief came and spoke; he said the Kuyui Dokado did not appreciate Numaga's overfriendliness with the Whites. Others appealed to him and one or two threatened him. Numaga was indifferent, for he had lost the desire to live.

After the Pyramid Lake wars, Numaga and Colonel F.W. Lander negotiated peace terms whereby Numaga was to keep his Indians close to the lake area.[281]

Albert Aleck

Albert Aleck was forty-three years old when, as chairman of the Tribal Council, he represented the Pyramid Lake group at the Congressional Hearings on S. 24, May 20 and 21, 1943.[282] He was born on the reservation; after his educational training at the Carson Indian School he returned to the reservation.

He knew the history of the squatters on the reservation, as he had heard the many stories of the old Indians in Wadsworth, and knew the Indians were ever hopeful that they would live to see the tribe regain their land from the white claimants. Mr. Aleck, with his firsthand knowledge of the conditions on the reservation, stood squarely to face the Congressmen, who were anxious to pass S. 24 that advocated giving the reservation lands to the white squatters.

He has consistently held other offices on the Tribal Council. Because he has been, and still is, reliable, hard working, and interested, he has held the chairmanship of the Pyramid Lake Tribal Council for many terms.

Tip Wadsworth
Tip Wadsworth was a singer who, by his songs, helped to keep alive the traditions of the Indians. Because of his unstinting service in leading the Indians in dance and song and ritual, he may be rated as a specialized leader as stated in Chapter II. In spite of the fact that he was blind, he always responded when asked to sing. Records of his songs have been made and help to perpetuate the Indian culture.

Summary
The leaders of the Pyramid Lake band met the challenges of their time. Truckee practiced his tribal training, friendliness, gentleness and courage in spite of rebuffs. His son, Winnemucca, preferred to stay away from the oncoming whites, though he had the same cultural training as his father. The practice of roving caused the government to place his band on reservations in Oregon and Washington. Sarah Winnemucca Hopkins was frustrated in most of her efforts to help her people; finally, she received aid to write about them and their forced adjustments to ease white pioneer travel and settlement in the West. Numaga realized the need to cooperate with the settlers, but his people did not always appreciate his friendliness with the whites. Captain Dave helped in the transition from self-disciplinary way of life (band culture) to the new form of law and order the group had to follow in the whites' cultural pattern. Albert Aleck lived at the time the band utilized the suffrage to voice the choice of county, state, and national leaders. Poignantly, in Washington, D.C., he faced the political friends and enemies of the Kuyui Dokado. In spite of the intercultural tribulations, there was song, play, dance, and ritual for the Kuyui Dokado, and Tip Wadsworth was one who helped the band to sing, dance, and carry on its ancient ritual.

CHAPTER XI

Summary

In the early-nineteenth-century, the Kuyui Dokado were apparently a happy band of Indians living near the shores of Pyramid Lake. Their life was very simple when Frémont contacted them. The band mode of life was one of self sufficiency; and they were at peace with the surrounding bands which were of the same tribal culture.

When the white pioneers began to cross the northern Paiute country on their way to California, there were some interethnic conflicts that led to disasters. For the most part the Indians were friendly, but the immigrants distrusted their friendship.

The semi-nomadic Paiute bands traditionally traveled among themselves over a wide area, but with the coming of the whites, they were asked to settle in distinct localities known as reservations. Many band Indians were unhappy to leave their ancestral homes, and many moved reluctantly, but they reasoned when they moved they could be free from the unfriendly immigrants and the gun-wielding soldiers. With the Paiute tribal exodus to reservations the shattered economy of the Kuyui Dokado band was insufficient. Though fish were plentiful, the plant food was inadequate for the needs of the Kuyui Dokado and other Paiutes who had come into the reservation. Those bands which refused to settle on a reservation in Nevada were moved to areas within the present states of Oregon, Washington, and Idaho. Because of these and other factors the old Paiutes counselled, "Keep this land and lake, because they are all we have left."

By the time white contacts were made in the Paiute area, Federal legislation had been developed to protect both Indians and whites. Early Americans had frequently practiced extermination of the Indians when they sought tribal lands, but conflicts in Nevada, though often bitter, were not as intense as in the East.

The Kuyui Dokado transition from their traditional culture and mode of living to the whites' mode has been slow. The Indians cling to old ways, but notice the necessity to make some changes in order to make physical life easier. The desire to keep the band entity, and to remain the Neh-muh (Indian) they are. Most of them prefer to be the Neh-muh in an Indian dominant area rather than move into predominant white zones. The Paiute language is still spoken in most of the Indian homes, especially where there are older people. The children are bilingual, though of late most understand the Paiute language but do not speak it.

The Kuyui Dokado prefer to live on the reservation and eke out a living rather than to move. Since there is no water for irrigation, farming is at a standstill. Because there can be no alfalfa for winter feeding of cattle, the cattle industry has practically disappeared. Thus many changes have been forced upon the group. Some men commute to neighboring towns to work, but as the quiet reservation land lends the desired atmosphere for rearing the children, they maintain their homes near the river and the lake.

Some of the younger ones, however, left to work not only in the towns of Nevada but also in California and other states. Many were disillusioned in the urban living and have returned to live on the reservation. The trend now is to force the federal recognition for need of equity in the tribal rights to water and land.

Appendix A

A record taken of crimes on the Pyramid Lake Reservation 1883-1905

Year	Arrests	Crime	Verdict and Sentence	Verified
1883	4	3 trivial,	reprimand,	Commissioner's
		1 assault	3 day guard house	Report, 1883
1886	14	3 intoxicated,	2 30-day jail	Commissioner's
		3 assault,	1 acquitted, 1 3-day jail plus 2 weeks' work in fields,	Report, 1886
		1 assault and battery,	30-day jail,	
		2 property damage,	1 acquitted, 1 convicted,	
		1 mother-in-law case,	10-minute jail,	
		1 divorce,	mutual consent,	
		3 rights of property of deceased	adjusted	
1888	3	1 wife beating,		Commissioner's
		1 horse killing,		Report, 1888
		1 murder	jailed in Carson	
1889	no serious crime			Commissioner's Report, 1890
1898	no serious crime			Report of the Dept. of Interior, 1898
1905	Decline of Wadsworth, no deputy			Report of the Dept. of Interior, 1906

Notes

1. Omer C. Stewart: The Northern Paiute Bands *Anthropological Records*, 2:3 (Berkeley), University of California Press, 1939, p. 138.
2. Scientific name (allium bisceptrum); Paiute name (pah duze)
3. Julian H. Steward, "Basin-Plateau Aboriginal-Sociopolitical Groups", *Ethnology Bulletin* 120 (Washington: U.S. Government Printing Office, 1938) pp. 263-272.
4. U.S. Congress, *Report of the Secretary of Interior,* Report 78, 43rd Congress, 1st Session, 1873-1874, Vol. 1, p. 697.
5. Stewart "The Northern Paiute Bands," *Anthropological Records,* Vol. 2, No. 3 (1939), p. 127.
6. Steward, "Basin-Plateau Aboriginal-Sociopolitical Groups", p. 5.
7. Willard S. Park and Others, "The Organization and Habitat of Paviotso Bands, in Tribal Distribution in the Great Basin", *American Anthropologists,* 40, (1938) p. 624.
8. U.S. Congress, *Report of the Secretary of Interior,* Report 157, 43rd Congress, 1st Session, 1873-1874, Vol. 1, p. 429.
9. Sam L. Rogers, *Indian Population in the United tales and Alaska,* (Washington: U.S. Government Printing Office, 1915), p. 96.
10. U.S. Congress, Department of the Interior, *Annual Report of the Commissioner of Indian Affairs (1883),* P· 110.
11. Stewart, "Northern Paiute", p. 362.
12. Rogers, *Indian Population in the United States and Alaska,* p.·96.
13. Stewart, "Northern Paiute" (map), p. 360.
14. Stewart, "Northern Paiute", p. 331.
15. Ibid., p. 373 .
16. Stewart, "Northern Paiute", p. 409.
17. Stewart, "Northern Paiute", p. 410.
18. Stewart, "Northern Paiute", P· 411.
19. *Ibid* ., p. 411.
20. *Interview* with Woozie George, told to Mrs. Wheat, Fallon, Nevada, 1960.
21. Stewart, "Northern Paiute", p. 405.
22. Stewart, "Northern Paiute", P· 373.
23. Ruth Murray Underhill, A History of Indians in the United States, (Chicago and London: The University o f Chicago Press, 1953), pp. 263, 266, 267.
24. Ruth Underhill, *The Northern Paiute Indians of California and Nevada,* (Lawrence, Kansas: Haskell Institute Printing Department, 1941), p. 52.
25. Frémont, Narratives, p. 424.
26. *Interview* with Lillie Shaw, July 24, 1960. Wadsworth. Nevada.

27.   Stewart, the Northern Paiute Bands, p. 42.

28.   Cora Du Bois, "The 1870 Ghost Dance", *Anthropological Papers,* Vol. 3 (Berkeley: University of California Press. 1956), p. 1.

29.   Dale L. Morgan, *Jedediah Smith,* (Lincoln: University of Nebraska Press, 1953), pp. 175, 210, 211, 213.

30.   Gloria Griffin Cline, *Exploring the Great Basin,* (Norman: University of Oklahoma Press, 1963), p. 123, 124.

31.   Peter Skene Ogden's Journal, 1828, Sunday, November 9.

32.   Ogden's Journal, 1828, Wednesday, November 19th.

33.   Ogden's Journal, 1829, Thursday, May 26.

34.   Ogden's Journal, 1829, Tuesday, June 7th.

35.   Ogden's Journal, 1829, Saturday, May 14th.

36.   Zenas Leonard, *Narratives,* 110-11.

37.   Gloria Griffin Cline: *Exploring the Great Basin,* p. 175.

38.   Washington Irving, *The Adventures of Captain Bonneville.* U.S.A. in the Rocky Mountains and the Far West (Norman: University of Oklahoma Press, 1961) pp. 283-296.

39.   Hiram Martin Chittenden, *The American Fur Trade of the Far West* (Stanford: Academic Reprints, 1954), p. 423.

40.   Zenas Leonard, *Narrative of the Adventures of Zenas Leonard* (Cleveland: The Burrows Brothers Company, 1940), p. 163.

41.   Ibid., p. 157.

42.   Allan Nevins, Fremont, *Pathmarker of the West* (New York: D. Appleton-Century Company, Inc., 1939), p. 69.

43.   John Charles Frémont, *Narratives of Exploration and Adventure* (New York: Longmans, Green and Company, 195), p. 187.

44.   Ibid., p. 308.

45.   Reno Evening Gazette, April 13, 1960. One of the Indian was the grandfather of John Hicks. John, a Shoshone-Cherokee, married a Paiute woman from Nixon, Nevada.

46.   Frémont, *Narratives,* pp. 309-311.

47.   Ibid., p. 332.

48.   Frémont, *Narratives,* p. 336.

49.   Frémont, *Narratives,* p. 336.

50.   Frémont, *Narratives,* p. 340. The Paiute name for this same rock is "Woh-noh" because of its shape; the lake is "Pah-nun-a-d," or "Coo yu ee Pah." One of the tufas found around Pyramid Lake, is the legendary "Stone Mother", which is situated on the eastern shore: it is the unhappy mother whose tears have made the lake. (*Interview* with Lillie Shaw: July 1960, Wadsworth, Nevada.)

51.   Frémont, *Narratives,* p. 340.

52.   Omer Stewart: "Culture Element Distribution: 14. Northern Paiute," *Anthropological Records,* 4 (April 3, 1941) p. 407.

53.   Margaret M. Wheat, *Survival Arts of the Primitive Paiutes.* (Reno : University of Nevada Press, 1968), pp. 109-111.

54.   Charles Preuss, *Exploring With Frémont* (Norman: University of Oklahoma Press, 1958), p. 104.

55. The Cutthroat trout has practically disappeared from Pyramid Lake and the Truckee River because the spawning condition have changed. There is little water in the river, and a dam for irrigation hinders the trout passage upstream. The trout are being planted in the lake but cannot reproduce.

56. John Charles Frémont, *Memoirs of My Life* (Chicago: Belford, Clark and Company, 1887), Vol. 1, p. 316.

57. *Ibid*, p. 312.

58. Frémont, *Narratives*, p. 342.

59. Frémont, *Narratives*, pp. 342- 343 .

60. Dan DeQuille (William Wright), *The Big Bonanza* (New York: Alfred A. Knopf, 194 7), p. 76.

61. DeQuille, *The Big Bonanza*, pp. 77-78.

62. U.S. Congress, Senate, *Report of the Secretary of the Interior*, 36th Congress, 1st Session, 1859-60, Vol. 1, Report 175, p. 741.

63. U.S. Congress, *Report of the Secretary of the Interior*, 1859-60, p. 742.

64. Myron Angel, ad. Reproduction of Thompson and West's "History of Nevada," 1881. With illustrations and Biographical Sketches of Its Prominent Men and Pioneers (Berkeley: Howell-North, 1958), pp. 150-151.

65. Angel, *History of Nevada*, p. 148.

66. *ibid.*, p. 150.

67. *ibid.*, p. 151.

68. Hubert Howe Bancroft, *History of Nevada, Colorado, and Wyoming* (San Francisco: The History Company, Publishers 1890) p. 208.

69. U.S. Congress, Senate, *Authorizing Patents Issued to Settlers Pyramid Lake Indian Reservation, Nevada*, Hearings before the Committee on Indian Affairs, 75th Congress, 1st Session on S. 840, Apr il 12, 13, and May 3, and 17, 1937, p. 98.

70. Bancroft, History of Nevada, p. 208.

71. William C. Miller, "The Pyramid Lake Indian War, 1860." Nevada Historical Society *Quarterly*, Part 1 (Carson City Printing Office, 1947), p. 37.

72. Daily Alta California, "The Beginning of the Battle of Pyramid Lake" (San Francisco: May 20, 1860), p. 2, col. 2.

73. David E.W. Williamson "When Major Ormsby was Killed" Nevada State Historical Society Papers, (1923-1924), 17.

74. *Daily Alta California*, "The Beginning of the Battle of Pyramid Lake" (San Francisco: May 20, 1860) p. 2, col. 2.

75. Williamson, "When Major Ormsby was Killed", pp. 16-24.

76. *Daily Alta California*, "An Interesting Letter from Carson Valley": Ira A. Eaton (San Francisco: May 18, 1860) , p. 1, Col. 2.

77. *Mountain Democrat,* (Editorial), (Placerville, California; May 18, 1860), Col. 1.

78. DeQuille, *The Big Bonanza*, p. 80.

79. Angel, History of Nevada, p. 150.

80. Miller, The Pyramid Lake Indian War, 1860 , Nevada Historical Society Quarterly, 2 (November, 1957), 107.

81. U.S., *Statutes at Large*, IV, 735.

82. *Ibid.*, IV, 564.

83. *Ibid.*, IX, 395.

84.   Elmer F. Bennett, *Federal Indian Law* (Washington: United States Printing Office), pp. 227-239.

85.   Charles J. Kappler, Indian Affairs, Laws, and Treaties (Washington: Government Printing Office, 1904) , Vol. J, 868.

86.   US, *Statutes at Large*, XLIII, 253.

87.   *Ibid.*, XL VIII, 596.

88.   U.S. *Statutes at Large*, LXVII, 98.

89.   Ibid., XLIX, 1757.

90.   Ibid., XLVIII, 984.

91.   Bennett, *Federal Indian Law,* p. 1, pp. 215-218.

92.   U.S. Congress, Senate, Report of the Secretary of the Interior, 36th Congress, 1st Session, 1859-60, p. 740.

93.   U.S. Congress, Report of the Secretary of the Interior, 36th Congress, p. 742.

94.   *Ibid.*, p 740.

95.   Kappler, *Indian Affairs, Laws, and Treaties,* p. 868. Old Indians recognized Agent Major Dodge as a friend and respectfully called him "Major." Later, in his memory, the reservation bench land west of the Truckee River between Wadsworth and Nixon was called Dodge Flat.

96.   U.S. Congress, Senate, *Senate Documents,* 1861-62, 2nd Session, 37th Congress, Vol. 1, Report 40, pp. 717-720.

97.   U.S. Congress, House of Representatives, Committee on Indian Affairs, *Pyramid Lake Reservation,* Hearings before the Committee, 78th Congress, 1st Session, on S. 24, April 12, 13, May 3 and 17, 1937, p. 42.

98.   U.S. Congress, House, 2nd Session, 43rd Congress, *Report of the Secretary of the Interior,* 1874-75, Vol. 1, p. 586.

99.   Kappler, Indian Affairs, Laws, and Treaties, 190 4, Vol. 1, p. 868.

100. U.S., *Statutes at Large,* XXXII, 388: Kappler, *Indian Affairs, Laws, and Treaties,* 1913, pp. 70-71.

101. U.S., *Statutes at Large*, XXXIX, 123.

102. *Ibid.*, XXXIX, 969.

103. *Ibid.*, XL, 561.

104. U.S. Congress, Department of Interior, *Report of the Commissioner of Indian Affairs,* 1866, p. 121.

105. Serial set No. 2379. United States Congress, Executive Documents, Report of the Secretary of the Interior, 1885-86, p. 373.

106. U.S., *Statutes at Large,* XLIII, 596.

107. James Shaw, letter to Superintendent Snyder, Wadsworth, Nevada, May 15, 1925. Nevada Indian Agency File, Stewart, Nevada.

108. U.S. *Statutes at Large,* XLIX, 787.

109. Pyramid Lake Tribal Council, letter to the Nevada Congressmen, Nixon, Nevada, April 23, 1935. (Nevada Indian Agency File, Stewart, Nevada).

110. U.S. of America, *plaintiff v. Garaventa Land and Livestock Co., a Corporalion et al: defendants.* U.S. District Court of Nevada, 38 F. Supp. 191.

111. *Ibid.*, 128F 2nd 416.

112. U.S. Congress, Senate Miscellaneous Reports. Report 80, 78th Congress, 1st Session, 1943 (Washington: Government Printing Office, 1943, p. 1.

113. U.S. Statutes at Large. XLVIH, 984.
114. The U.S. of America, plaintiff v. Orr Water Ditch Company, et al; defendants, Carson City (Washington: Government Printing Office 1944).
115. Dillon Myers, letter to Superintendent, Carson Indian Agency, Stewart, Nevada, 1951.
116. U.S. *Statutes al Large,* LX, 1959.
117. *Ibid., Reno Evening Gazette,* Indian Claims are Established April 16, 1959, p. 28, Col. 1.
118. Steward, "Basin-Plateau Aboriginal Sociopolitical Groups", p. 4.
119. U.S. Congress, Senate, Senate Documents. Vol. 1, 1859-60, p. 743.
120. U.S. Congress, House, Reports of the• Secretary of the Interior and Postmaster General. 2nd Session, 38th Congress, 1864-65, p. 283.
121. U.S. Congress, House, Reports of the Secretary of the Interior, 1872-73, Vol. 1, 3rd Session, 42nd Congress , p. 66
122. *Ibid.,* p. 447.
123. U.S. Congress, Executive Document. 3rd Session, 46ᵗʰ Congress, 1880-81, Vol. 9, p. 93
124. *Ibid.,* p. 246.
125. U.S. Congress, Department of the Interior, *Annual Report of the Commissioner of Indian Affairs.* 1885, p. 142.
126. U.S. Congress, Department of the Interior, *Report of the Commissioner of Indian Affairs.* 1881, p. 132.
127. *Ibid.,* 1883, p. 110.
128. *Ibid.,* 1885, p. 142.
129. *Ibid.,* 1886, p. 195.
130. *Ibid.,* 1888, p. 180.
131. U.S. Congress, Report of the Secretary of the Interior, 1896, Vol. 2, p. 207.
132. U.S. Congress, Department of the Interior, Report of the Commissioner of Indian Affairs. 1899, p. 239.
133. U.S. Congress, Pyramid Lake Indian Reservation. Hearings before the Committee on Indian Affairs, House of Representatives, 78th Congress, 1st session on Senate Bill 24, May 20 and 21, 1943, p. 33.
134. Glen D. Fulcher, *An Economic Analysis of the Alternative Uses for the Truckee River Allotted to the Pyramid Lake Indians.* (Reno: University of Nevada, Agricultural Economics Department, 1959), p. 4.
135. U.S. Congress, Senate, Report of the Secretary of the Interior. 36th Congress, 1st Session, 1859-60, p. 742.
136. U.S. Congress, Senate, *Senate Documents,* 1861-1862, 2nd Session, 37th Congress, Vol. 1, Report 40, p. 719.
137. U.S. Congress, Report of the Secretary of the Interior, 1864-65, p. 287.
138. U.S. Congress, 38th Congress, Department of the Interior. Annual Report on Indian affairs by the Acting Commissioner, 1867, pp. 168-170.
139. U.S. Congress, Department of the Interior, Annual Report on Indian Affairs by the Acting Commissioner, 1867, p. 170.
140. *Ibid.,* p. 172.
141. U.S. Congress, *Report of the Secretary of the Interior,* 1868-69, 3rd Session, 40th

Congress, p. 605 .

142. U.S. Congress, *Executive Documents,* 2nd Session, 42nd Congress, 1871-72 Vol. 1, p. 976.

143. U.S. Congress, *Report of the Secretary of the Interior,* 1873-74, p. 586.

144. *Ibid.,* 1878, Vol.1, p. 598.

145. U.S. Congress, Department of the Interior, *Report of the Commissioner of Indian Affairs,* 1881, p. 131.

146. U.S. Congress, House, Executive Documents, 2nd Session, 53rd Congress, Vol. 14, *Report of the Secretary of the Interior,* Vol. 2, 1893, p. 206.

147. U.S. Congress, *Report of the Secretary of the Interior.* 1899, p. 238.

148. U.S., *Statutes at Large,* XXXVI, 269.

149. Ibid XXXIX, 123.

150. U.S. Congress, *Executive documents.* House, 2nd Session 46th Congress, 1879-80, Vol. 9, pp. 215-216.

151. U.S. Congress, Department of the Interior, *Report of the Commissioner of Indian Affairs,* 1881. p. 190.

152. U.S. Congress, Department of the Interior, *Report of the Commissioner of Indian Affairs.* 1885, p. 142.

153. *Ibid.,* 1887, p. 165.

154. *Ibid.,* 1889, p. 250.

155. U.S. Congress, House, *Executive Documents,* Report of the Secretary of the Interior, 1st Session, 52nd Congress, Vol. 2, 1891, p. 298.

156. U.S. Congress, Report of the Secretary of the Interior, 1903, p. 245.

157. *Ibid.,* 1905, p. 272.

158. U.S. Congress, *Authorizing Patents Issued to Settlers, Pyramid Lake Indian Reservation, Nevada,* p. 65.

159. U.S. Congress, Pyramid Lake Indian Reservation, Committee Hearings, House of Representatives, S. 24, (Government Printing Office, 1943) p. 23.

160. *Ibid.,* p. 30.

161. *Ibid.,* p. 27.

162. Glen D. Fulcher, "An Economic Analysis of the Alternative Uses for the Truckee River Water Allotted to the Pyramid Lake Indians" (Reno: University of Nevada Agricultural Economic Department, 1959), p. 4.

163. Fulcher, "Economic Analysis", p. 8. About 841 head of cattle on the reservation were owned by 48 farmers. 35 owners had 1-10 head; 4 owners had 10-20 head; 3 owners had 20-30 head; 2 owners had 30-40 head; 2 owners had 40-50 head; 2 owners had 50-75 head.

164. *Ibid.,* p. 10.

165. U.S. Congress, Senate, *Senate Documents,* No. 42, 1873-74, Vol. 1, p. 5.

166. U.S. Congress, *Report of the Secretary of the Interior,* 1865-66, p. 309.

167. *Ibid.,* 1880-81, p. 246.

168. U.S. Congress, Department of the Interior, *Report of the Commissioner of Indian Affairs,* 1889, p. 249.

169. Interview with Daisy Astor (Choo-du), July 1, 1959, Wadsworth, Nevada.

170. U.S Congress, *Report of the Secretary of the Interior* 1872-73, p. 467.

171. U.S. Congress, Department of the Interior, *Report of the Commissioner of Indian*

Affairs, 1880, p. 216.

172. *Ibid.*, 1890, p. 148.

173. U.S. Congress, House, *Executive Documents.* 1893-94, 2nd Session, 53 Cong., Vol. 14, p. 210.

174. Interview with Daisy Astor (Choo-du), July 1, 1959, Wadsworth, Nevada.

175. U.S. Congress, Department of the Interior, 1905, p. 256.

176. Sarah Winnemucca Hopkins, *Life Among the Piutes* (New York: G.P. Putnam, 1883), p. 67.

177. U.S. Congress, *Senate Documents*, 2nd Session, 37th Congress, Vol. 1, 1861-62, p. 719.

178. U.S. Congress, *Senate Documents*, 2nd Session, 37th Congress, Vol. 1, 1861-62, p. 723.

179. U.S. Congress, *Report of the Secretary of the Interior*, 1871-72, 2nd Session, 42nd Congress, p. 975.

180. *Ibid.*, 1878-79, Vol. 9, p. III.

181. *Ibid.*, p. 598.

182. U.S. Congress, Department of the Interior, *Annual Report of the Commissioner of Indian Affairs,* 1891, p. 302.

183. U.S. Congress, Executive Documents, House, 3rd Sess., 46th Cong., 1880-81. Vol. 9, p. 247.

184. U.S. Congress, Department of the Interior, *Annual Report of the Commissioner of Indian Affairs,* 1880, p. 216.

185. Ibid., 1883, p. 110.

186. U.S. Congress, Department of the Interior, *Annual Report of the Commissioner of Indian Affairs,* 1885, p. 142.

187. Ibid., 1886, p. 196.

188. Ibid., 1888, p. 180.

189. Ibid., 1886, p. 195.

190. U.S. Congress, Department of the Interior, *Annual Report of the Commissioner of Indian Affairs*, 1887, p. 163.

191. J.G. Scrugham, *Nevada, A Narrative of the Conquest of a Frontier Land* (Chicago: The American Historical Society, Inc., 1935), 1 :348, 149.

192. C. Leon Wall, "Indian Education in Nevada, 1861-1951" Thesis (Reno: University of Nevada, 1962), p. 28.

193. U.S. Congress, Department of the Interior, *Report of the Commissioner of Indian Affairs,* 1890, p. 147.

194. U.S. Congress, Interior Department, *Message and Documents*, Vol. 2, 1891-92, p. 302.

195. *Ibid.*, p. 301.

196. U.S. Congress, Department of the Interior, *Report of the Commissioner of Indian Affairs*, 1893, p. 209.

197. U.S. Congress, Report of the Department of Interior 1899, p. 239.

198. Wall, *Indian Education in Nevada*, Table X, Appendix.

199. Haglund, E.A., The Washoe, Paiute, and Shoshone Indians of Nevada (Carson City, Nevada: State Printing Office, 1961), p. 23.

200. U.S. Congress, *Senate Documents*, 2nd Session, 37th Congress, 1861-62, pp. 365, 359, 362.

201. U.S. Congress, *Report of the Secretary of the interior,* 1878-79, Vol. 9, p. 599.
202. U.S. Congress, Department of the Interior, Report of the Commissioner of Indian Affairs, 1880, p. 123.
203. *Ibid.,* 1881, p. 131.
204. U.S. Congress, Department of the Interior, Report of the Commissioner of Indian Affairs, 1891, p. 300.
205. *Ibid.,* 1883, p. 110.
206. *Ibid.,* 1888, p. 182.
207. *Ibid.,* 1891, p. 300.
208. *Ibid.,* 1889, p. 250.
209. Appendix A.
210. U.S. *Statutes at Large,* XLVII, 336.
211. U.S. Congress, *Senate Documents,* 2nd Session, 37th Congress, 1861-62, p. 723.
212. U.S. Congress, Department of the Interior, *Report of the Commissioner of Indian Affairs,* 1866, p. 115.
213. U.S. Congress, *Report of the Secretary of the Interior.* 2nd Session, 41st Congress, 1869-70, p. 644.
214. U.S. Congress, *Report of the Secretary of the Interior,* 1874, p. 432.
215. U.S. Congress, Department of the Interior, *Report of the Commissioner of Indian Affairs,* 1886, p. 196.
216. *Ibid.,* 1887, p. 165.
217. U.S. Congress, Report of the Secretary of the Interior, 1878-79, Vol. 9, p. 599.
218. U.S. Congress, Department of the Interior, Report of the Commissioner of Indian Affairs, 1886, p. 196.
219. *Ibid.,* 1889, p. 249.
220. U.S. Statutes at Large, XXXVIII, 1228.
221. *Ibid* .. XLIII, 1141.
222. U.S. *Statutes at Large,* XLIV, 453.
223. *Ibid.,* XLIV, 934.
224. U.S. Congress, Department of the Interior, Appropriation Bill, 1935.
225. Janette Woodruff and Cecil Dryden, *Indian Oasis,* (Caldwell, Idaho: Caxton Printers, Ltd., 1939), p. 276.
226. U.S. *Statutes at Large,* LXVII, 568.
227. U.S. Congress, *Indians on Federal Reservations in the United States* (Washington: Government Printing Office, 1961), pp. 47-48.
228. The 1870 Ghost Dance by Cora Du Bois, Pages 1-8.
229. U.S. Congress, *Report of the Secretary of the Interior,* 1871-72, 2nd Session, 42nd Congress, p. 671.
230. U.S. Congress, Department of the Interior, *Report of the Commissioner of Indian Affairs,* 1875. p. 172.
231. Ibid., 1887, p. 165.
232. U.S. Congress, Executive Documents, Report of the Secretary of the Interior, 1893-94, p. 211.
233. George W. Smart, "Mission to Nevada, A History of Nevada Indian Missions", Unpublished Dissertation, Central Baptist Theological Seminary (Lawrence, Kansas: Haskell Institute Printing Office, 1958), pp. 78, 97.

234. Woodruff and Dryden, *Indian Oasis,* pp. 208-209.

235. Smart, "Mission to Nevada", p. 97. Father Hogben was the only minister on the Pyramid Lake Reservation to learn the Paiute language. In his sermons he used Paiute phrases and words for emphasis. The Indians were very pleased to have him do this.

236. Smart, "Mission to Nevada", p. 99.

237. Smart, "Mission to Nevada", Appendix B.

238. *Ibid.,* p. 80.

239. Richard Evans Shutler, "The Appeal of Peyote as a Medicine" Leslie Spier (Editor), *American Anthropologists* (Menasha, Wisconsin: The American Anthropological Association, 1938, p. 698.

240. Smart, "Mission to Nevada", p. 116.

241. Omer Call Stewart, Washo-Northern Paiute Peyotism (Berkley: California University Printing Office, 1944), pp. 68, 61, p. 130.

242. Interview with Daisy Astor, Edith Shaw and Lillie Sim, Wadsworth, Nevada; 1959.

243. U.S. Congress, *Report of the Secretary of the Interior,* 1941, p. 410.

244. U.S. Congress, *Report of the Secretary of the Interior,* 1942, p. 237.

245. U.S. Congress, *Hearings Before the Committee on Indian Affairs,* Pyramid Lake Reservation, House of Representative on S. 24, 78th Congress, 1st Session, May 20 and 21, 1943, p. 19.

246. U.S. Congress, *Hearings Before the Committee on Indian Affairs,* Pyramid Lake Reservation, House of Representative on S. 24, 78th Congress, 1st Session, May 20 and 21, 1943, p. 24.

247. *The Examiner, The American Weekly.* "Star in the Desert" (San Francisco: February 3, 1952), p. 4.

248. *Nevada State Journal,* "Posthumous Decoration to P.F. Shaw" (Reno: January 6, 1944), p. 12, Col. 3..

249. *The Nevada Legionnaire,* "Nevada's Most Decorated Service Man Dies" (Sparks: June 1957), p. 1, Col. 6-7.

250. *The Examiner: The American Weekly.* "Star in the Desert" (San Francisco: February 3, 1952), p. 5.

251. *Nevada State Journal,* "All-American A.W.V.S. Unit Formed" (Reno: October 27, 1957), p. 3, Col. 1.

252. Carson Nevada Appeal. "Governor Charles H. Russell (picture)" (Carson City: February 20, 1958), Col. 1, p. 1.

253. U.S. *Statutes at Large,* LXII, 757 (1953).

254. Sarah Winnemucca Hopkins, Life Among the Piutes (New York: G.P. Putnam, 1883), pp. 5-6.

255. George R. Stewart, *The California Trail* (New York: McGraw-Hill Book Co., Inc., 1962), p. 33.

256. *Ibid.,* p. 69.

257. Sarah Winnemucca Hopkins, *Life Among the Piutes* (New York: G.P. Putnam, 1883), pp. 8, 10, 27.

258. *Ibid.,* pp. 18, 20, 27, 43, 69.

259. [259] Sarah Winnemucca Hopkins, Life Among the Piutes (New York: G.P. Putnam, 1883), p. 67.

260. *Ibid.*, pp. 11, 13, 15.
261. Executive Documents (Washington: Government Printing Office, 1860), p. 742.
262. Frederick Webb Hodge, *Handbook of American Indians North of Mexico*, (New York: Pageant Books, Inc., 1950), p. 962.
263. *Executive Documents*, Washington: Government Printing Office, 1863), p. 365.
264. *Ibid.*, 1861-62, p. 718.
265. Sarah Winnemucca Hopkins, *Life Among the Piutes* (New York: G.P. Putnam, 1883), p. 105.
266. Louis Wolfe, *Indians Courageous*, (New York: Dodd, Mead & Company, 1956), pp. 101, 103, 115.
267. *Report of the Secretary of the Interior*, 18 80-81 (Washington: Government Printing Office, 1881), p. 26.
268. Sarah Winnemucca Hopkins, *Life Among the Piutes* (New York: G.P. Putnam, 1883), p. 193.
269. Hubert Howe Bancroft, *History of Nevada, Colorado, and Wyoming,* (San Francisco: The History Company, Publishers, 1890), p. 222.
270. Sarah Winnemucca Hopkins, *Life Among the Piutes* (New York: G.P. Putnam, 1883), p. 3.
271. *Ibid.*, pp. 5, 46, 134.
272. California *Historical Society Quarterly*, Dr. J.J.F. Haine, "A Belgian in the Gold Rush: California Indians" (San Francisco: Society Publishers, 1959), Vol. XXXVIII, pp. 135, 154, 155.
273. Frederick w. Hodge, *Handbook of American Indians North of Mexico,* (New York: Pageant Books, Inc., 1959), p. 962.
274. Sarah Winnemucca Hopkins, *Life Among the Piutes* (New York: G.P. Putnam, 1883), pp. 96, 98.
275. Janette Woodruff- Cecil Dryden, *Indian Oasis* (Caldwell, Idaho: The Caxton Printers. 1939), p. 162.
276. *Report of the Commissioner of Indian Affairs,* (Washington: Government Printing Office, 1888), pp. 183. Numana (Neh-muh-nah) is Paiute interpreted the Indians father or leader.
277. Thompson and West, *History of Nevada,* 1881, (Berkeley, Howell and North, 1958), p. 151.
278. James G. Scrugham, History of Nevada, (Chicago: The American Historical Society, Inc., Vol. 1, 1935), p. 139.
279. Sarah Winnemucca Hopkins, *Life Among the Piutes,* (New York: G.P. Putnam, 1883), p. 60.
280. Thompson and West, *History of Nevada,* 1881, (Berkeley, Howell and North, 1958), p. 151.
281. James G. Scrugham, *History of Nevada* (Chicago: The American Historical Society, Inc., 1935), p. 142.
282. *Pyramid Lake Indian Reservation,* Hearings Before the Committee on Indian Affairs, House of Representatives, S. 24 (Washington: Government Printing Office, 1943), p. 29.

Bibliography

Public Documents

U.S. Congress:

Executive Documents. House, 2nd Sess., 42nd Congress. 1871-72. Vol. I.

Executive Documents. House, 2nd Sess., 45th Congress. 1877-78. Vol. 8.

Executive Documents. House, 2nd Sess., 46th Congress. 1879-80. Vol. 9.

Executive Documents. House, 3rd Sess., 46th Congress. 1880-81. Vol. 9.

Executive Documents. House, 1st Sess., 49th Congress. 1885-86. Vol. 12.

Executive Documents. House, 1st Sess., 52nd Congress. 1891-92. Vol. 15.

Executive Documents. House, 2nd Sess., 53rd Congress. 1893-94. Vol. 14.

Indians on Federal Reservations in the United States, Washington Government Printing Office, 1961.

Senate, *Senate Documents,* 1861-62, 2nd Sess., 37th Congress. Vol. I. Report 40.

Senate, *Senate Documents,* 1873-74. Vol. I, Report 42.

Messages and Documents, Vol. 2. 1891-92.

Senate Miscellaneous Reports. 78th Congress, Ist Sess. 1943. Report 80.

Senate, *Authorizing Patents Issued to Settlers, Pyramid Lake Indian Reservation,* Nevada, Hearings Before the Committee on Indian Affairs. 75th Congress, 1st Sess. on S. 840, April 12, 13, and May 3 and 17, 1937.

House of Representatives, Committee on Indian Affairs. Pyramid Lake Reservation. Hearings before the Committee, 78th Congress. 1st Sess. on S. 24, April 12, 13, May 13 and 17, 1937.

Report of the Secretary of the Interior:

Senate, 36th Congress, 1st Sess. 1859-60. Report 175. Vol. 1.

House. (Report or the Secretary or Interior and Postmaster General), 38th Congress, 2nd Sess., 1864-65.

House, 39th Congress, 1st Sess., 1865-66.

House, 40th Congress. 3rd Sess., 1868-69.

House, 41st Congress, 2nd Sess., 1869-70.

House. 42nd Congress, 3rd Sess., 1872-73, Vol. 1.

House, 43rd Congress, 1st Sess ., 1873-74, Reports 78 and 157.

House, 44rd Congress, 2nd Sess., 1874-75, Vol. 1.

House, 45th Congress, 3rd Sess., 1878-79, Vol. 9.

House, 54th Congress. 2nd Sess., 1896-1897, Vol. 18.

House, 56th Congress, 1st Sess., 1899-1900, Vol. 18.

House, 1903, 1905, 1941, 1942.

Washington: Government Printing Office, 1860-1942.

Report of the Commissioner of Indian Affairs:
    1866, 1867, 1875, 1880, 1881, 1883, 1885, 1886, 1887, 1888, 1889, 1890, 1891,
    1893, 1899, Washington: Government Printing
Office, 1866-1899.

*U.S. of America, Plaintiff v. Garavanta Land and Livestock Company, A Corporation et
    al, Defendants,* No. 2741. (38F. Supp. 191) (128 F, 2nd 416)

U.S. of America, Plaintiff v. Orr Water Ditch Company, et al, Defendants, Carson City.
    Washington: Government Printing Office 1944.

U.S. Statutes at Large:
    Vols. XXIV, XXXIII, XXXVI, XXXVIII, XXXIX, XL, XLI, XLIII, XLIV, XLVII,
    SLVIII, XLIX, LX, LXVII.

State of Nevada

Haglund, E.A., "The Washoe, Paiute, and Shoshone Indians of Nevada", State
    Department of Education (Carson City: State Printing Office, 1961).

Miller, William C., "The Pyramid Lake Indian War, 1860", Nevada Historical
    Society *Quarterly*, 1 (1957), p. 37.

-------· "The Pyramid Lake Indian War, 1860", Nevada Historical Society *Quarterly*,
    2 (November, 1957), p. 107.

Williamson, E.W., "When Major Ormsby was Killed", Nevada State Historical
    Society *Papers*, 4 (1923-24), 17.

Books

Angel, Myron, ed. Reproduction of Thompson and West's "History of Nevada", 1881.
    With Introduction by David F. Myrick. Berkeley, California: Howell-North,
    1958. 680 pp.

Bancroft, Hubert Howe. *History of Nevada, Colorado, and Wyoming,* 1540-1888. San
    Francisco: The History Company, Publishers, 1890.

-------· *History of California,* V. 4, 1840-1845. San Francisco: A.L. Bancroft and
    Company, 1886.

Bennett, Elmer F. *Federal Indian Law.* Washington: United States Printing Office,
    1958.

Chittenden, Hiram Martin. *The American Fur Trade of the Far West.* Stanford:
    Academic Reprints, 1954.

Cleland, Robert G. *From Wilderness to Empire.* New York: A.A. Knopf, 1934.

Cline, Gloria Griffen. *Exploring the Great Basin.* Norman: University of Oklahoma
    Press, 1963.

Conner, David Ellis. *Joseph Reddeford Walker and the Arizona Adventure.* Norman:
    University of Oklahoma Press, 1956.

Coues, Elliott. *On the Trail of a Spanish Pioneer, The Diary and Itinerary of Francisco
    Garces.* Vol. 1. New York: Francis P. Harper, 1900.

Davis, Sam P. *History of Nevada.* Reno: The Elms Publishing Company, Inc. 1913.

Du Bois, Cora. "The 1870 Ghost Dance." *Anthropological Records.* Vol. 3. Berkeley:
    University of California Press, 1946.

Frémont, Jessie Benton. *The Origin of the Frémont Explorations*. Vol. XIX. London: The Century Company, 1890-91.

Frémont, John Charles. *Memoirs of My Life*. Vol. I. Chicago: Belford, Clark and Company, 1887.

_____. Narratives of Exploration and Adventure. New York: Longmans, Green and Company, 1956.

Hodge, Frederick Webb. Handbook of American Indians North of Mexico. New York: Pageant Books, Inc., 1950.

Hopkins, Sarah Winnemucca. *Life Among the Piutes*. New York· G.P. Putnam, 1883.

Irving, Washington. *The Adventures of Captain Bonneville in the Rocky Mountains and the Far West*. Norman: University of Oklahoma Press, 1961.

Kappler, Charles J. *Indian Affairs, Laws, and Treaties*. Washington: Government Printing Office, 1904.

Leonard, Zenas. *Narrative of the Adventures of Zenas Leonard*. Cleveland: The Burrows Brothers Company, 1904.

Morgan, Dale L. *The Great Salt Lake*. New York: Bobbs-Merrill Company. 1947.

Morgan, Dale L. *Jedediah Smith*. Lincoln: University of Nebraska Press. 1953.

Murphey, Edith Van Allen. Indian Uses of Native Plants. Palm Desert: Desert Printers, Inc., 1959.

Nevins, Allan. Frémont, Pathmarker of the West. New York: D. Appleton-Century Company. Inc. 1939.

Park, Willard Z. "The Organization and Habitat of Paviotso Bands in Tribal Distribution in the Great Basin," *American Anthropologists*, 40 (October-December 1938), 622-638.

Preuss, Charles. *Exploring with Frémont*. Norman: University of Oklahoma Press, 1958.

Rogers, Sam L. *Indian Population in the United States and Alaska*. Washington: Government Printing Office, 1915.

Scrugham, James G. Nevada, *A Narrative of the Conquest of a Frontier Land*. Chicago: The American Historical Society. Inc. 1935.

Shutler, Richard Evans. "The Appeal or Peyote as a Medicine." *American Anthropologists*. Menasha, Wisconsin: The American Anthropological Association, 1938.

Steward, Julian. "Basin-Plateau Aboriginal Sociopolitical Groups." *Ethnology Bulletin* 120.

Stewart, George R. *The California Trail*. New York: McGraw-HiII Book Company, Inc., 1962.

Stewart. Omer. "Culture Element Distribution: 14. Northern Piaute". *Anthropological Records*, 4 (April 3, 1941), 361-446.

_____. "The Northern Paiute Bands", *Anthropological Records*. Vol. 2, No. 3, 1939.

_____. "Washo-Northern Paiute Peyotism. A Study in Acculturation." Vol. 40, No. 3, 1944.

Underhill, Ruth. Tire Northern Paiute Indians of California and Nevada. Lawrence, Kansas: Haskell Institute Printing Department, 1941.

_____. A History of Indians in the United States. Chicago and London: The University of Chicago Press, 1953.

Wheat, Margaret. "Notes on Paviotso Material Culture." Nevada State Museum Anthropological Papers, No. I. 1959.
Woodruff, Janelle and Cecil Dreydcn. *Indian Oasis.* Caldwell, Idaho The Caxton Printers, 1939.
Wright, William (Dan DeQuille). *The Big Bonanza* New York Alfred A. Knopf, 1947.

Periodicals
Bruce, lram Irene. "Legend of Pyramid lake". *Catholic World,* 154:597.8f42. 1942.
"Nevada's Most Decorated Service Man Die,." *The Nevada Legionnaire,* June 1957

Unpublished Material

Nevada Indian Agency File, Stewart, Nevada.
Letter from Hon. Dillon Meyers. Commissioner of Indian Affairs. Washington. D.C. 1951.

Letter from Pyramid Lake Tribal Council to Nevada Congressmen. Nixon, Nevada. April 23, 1935.

Letter from James Shaw, Pyramid Lake Indian. Wadsworth, Nevada, May 15, 1925.

Records of Saint Mary's Episcopal Church, Nixon. Nevada.

Theses and Dissertations:
Fulcher, Glen D. "An Economic Analysis, of the Alternative Uses for the Truckee River Allotted to the Pyramid Lake Indians" Unpublished dissertation, Reno: University of Nevada, Agricultural Economics Department, 1959.

Smart, George W. "Mission to Nevada. A History of Nevada Indian Missions," Unpublished dissertation. Central Baptist Theological Seminary, Lawrence, Kansas: Haskell Insitute Printing Office, 1958.

Wall, C. Leon. "Indian Education in Nevada, 1861-1951. "Unpublished Master's dissertation, Department of Education, University of Nevada, 1952.

Newspapers
Carson Nevada Appeal. February 20, 1958.
Daily Alta California. (San Francisco) May 18, 1860. May 20, 1860
Mountain Democrat. (Editorial) (Placerville, California): May 19, 1860
Nevada State Journal. (Reno) January 6, 1944, October 27, 1957.
Reno Evening Gazette. (Nevada) April 16, 1959, April 13, 1960.

Interviews
With Daisy Astor, Edith Shaw, and Lillie Shaw. Wadsworth, Nevada, 1959.
With Daisy Astor, Wadsworth, Nevada, July 1959.
With Woozie George and Mrs. Wheat, Fallon, Nevada, 1960.
With Lillie Shaw, Wadsworth, Nevada. July, 1960.

Acknowledgments

In appreciation to the many persons who encouraged me to publish this documentation of the Pyramid Lake Paiute People, and especially to the older Neh-muh who were anxious to have a recordation of their early history and tribal lore.

To Sessions S. (Buck) Wheeler for the fine tribute he gave the Paiutc People and me in the foreword. We have always appreciated his continued interest.

The early pictures of the transition of the Indians were taken by photographers, Mrs. Dick Cowles, Sr., and Harry Huston of Wadsworth, Nevada. They are remembered here for having had the interest and foresight to pictorially record the early life of the Paiutes.

Index

Note: Figures are indicated by *f* following the page number. End note information is indicated by n and note number following the page number.

Congressional Act (1932), 62
Coo-yu-ee Pah. *See* Pyramid Lake
Coo-yu-e Hoop (Salmon River), 38, 44
courts, federal, 62
Cowles, Dick, 46*f*
Creel, Mr., 63*f*
crimes, 62, 83. *See also* law and order; police
Crip, George, 29
cultural issues
 feasts and celebrations as, 3, 26, 63–64, 76
 intruders and white culture as, 14, 30,
  32–33, 40, 44, 81–82
 Kuyui Dokado band cultural
  background, 8–14
 legends and lore as, 4–7, 39, 85n50
 medical care and, 12, 63–64
 religious or spiritual practices as (*see*
  religious or spiritual practices)
 social change as (*see* social change)
 Wadsworth's songs on, 80

dams, 24, 47, 49, 50, 79
Dave (Numana/Captain), 2*f,* 37*f,* 38, 60*f,* 62,
  78–79, 80
Davidson, Robert A., 38
Davis, Jeff, 40
Davis, Jim, 51
Dawes Act (1887), 32–33
Dewey, Jim, 70
divorce, 11
Dodge, Frederick, 26, 27, 29, 35, 38, 44, 49,
  76, 87n95
Dodge Flat, 52, 87n95
droughts, 45, 49
Du Bois, Cora, 65–66
Dwight, T. T., 49

economic development, 44–55
 agriculture and, 44–45, 49–53, 82,
  89n163
 Central Pacific Railroad and, 44, 45,
  53–55, 54*f,* 59
 federal legislation on, 34, 54–55
 fishing and, 44–49, 45*f*–48*f*
 intruders effects on, 25, 44, 45, 47,
  51–53, 81

education, 33–34, 51, 56–59, 58*f,* 75
Elliot, A. B., 27
entrymen in the reservation, 38–43. *See also*
  intruders and invaders
Erb, Jim, 46*f*

families
 children in (*see* children)
 legends and lore about, 4–7, 39, 85n50
 matchmaking and marriage in, 3, 11
 mother as head of, 6, 9
 reunions of, 3
federal courts, 62
federal legislation, 31–36, 41–43, 54–55, 62,
  64–65, 70, 81
fires, 3, 4, 16, 66
fish
 bands affiliated with, 1, 3
 boats to catch, 47
 dam effects on, 24, 47, 49
 economic development tied to, 44–49,
  45*f*–48*f*
 permits to catch, 49
 in Pyramid Lake, 1, 9, 22–23, 47–49,
  48*f,* 86n55
 in Pyramid Lake Indians' diet, 9, 12, 17,
  22–23, 26, 45
 trading of, 17, 22, 39, 45–47, 45*f*–46*f*
 in Truckee River, 9, 17, 26, 47, 49, 86n55
 in Winnemucca Lake, 39, 47
Fitzpatrick, Thomas, 20
food resources
 education and, 56, 59
 farming of (*see* agriculture and farming)
 fish as (*see* fish)
 health and, 63
 intruders and, 15–17, 25, 26–27
 leaders' role in acquiring, 76
 on Northern Paiute land, 1, 3–4, 25
 Pyramid Lake Indian diet of, 9, 12,
  15–17, 22–23, 25–27, 39, 45, 49–50, 63
 reservation limitations of, 25, 29, 44,
  49–50, 81
Forney, J., 35
Frank, Robert, 40
Frazier, Eugene, 63*f*

About the Author

Nellie Shaw Harnar, a Neh-muh (Paiute Indian), was born in Wadsworth, Nevada, on the Pyramid Lake Reservation to James and Margie Shaw. One of nine children, her early childhood was filled with the activities of a large family and attending day school. Memorable pasttimes were the excursions to the Truckee River to swim, fish, gather berries, and play. Another favorite pasttime was listening to the male elders sing songs and tell of the tribal lore as they made their rabbit skin blankets, fish nets, and moccasins.

All too soon, Nellie had to forsake the security and comfort of home for most of each year to obtain an elementary education at the Carson Indian school, Stewart, Nevada. She graduated from Carson City High School and the Normal Training Course at Haskell Institute, Lawrence, Kansas. She obtained an AB Degree from Northern Arizona University, Flagstaff, Arizona, and an MA Degree from the University of Nevada, Reno. During this time she was busy teaching, married and raised one son, Curtis, Jr. With her formal education Mrs. Harnar retained her fluency of the Paiute Language.

She was baptized and confirmed in the Wadsworth Episcopal Church, which is now known as the St. Michaels and All Angels.

After 37 years as a teacher and Counselor in the BIA schools, she and her husband, Curtis Sequoyah Harnar, Sr., resided at Wadsworth until his death in the summer of 1978 enjoying their retirement amidst the tranquility and beauty of the Pyramid Lake Reservation.